Democracy versus Solidarity in the EU Discourse

Studies in European Integration, State and Society

Edited by Magdalena Góra,
Zdzisław Mach and Katarzyna Zielińska

Vol. 1

PETER LANG

Frankfurt am Main · Berlin · Bern · Bruxelles · New York · Oxford · Warszawa · Wien

Józef Niżnik

Democracy versus Solidarity in the EU Discourse

PETER LANG

Internationaler Verlag der Wissenschaften

Bibliographic Information published by the Deutsche Nationalbibliothek
The Deutsche Nationalbibliothek lists this publication in the Deutsche Nationalbibliografie; detailed bibliographic data is available in the internet at http://dnb.d-nb.de.

Cover Design:
© Olaf Gloeckler, Atelier Platen, Friedberg

ISSN 2193-2352
ISBN 978-3-631-63877-4

© Peter Lang GmbH
Internationaler Verlag der Wissenschaften
Frankfurt am Main 2012
All rights reserved.

www.peterlang.de

Contents

Preface

The current volume has been built out of texts which I have written over several years while working in the Institute of Philosophy and Sociology at the Polish Academy of Sciences on the European integration discourse. Therefore, its different parts were presented at international conferences and some of them published in collective volumes. Most of Chapters 1 and 7 were published in books edited by Josef Langer for Peter Lang publishing house (Niżnik, Józef, 2008, 2011a). Part of Chapter 2, has been published in a book edited by Marion Ellison for Policy Press (Niżnik, Józef, 2011b). Most of Chapter 4 has appeared in a book edited by Carlo Mongardini for Bulzoni Editore (Niżnik, Józef, 2002), and Chapter 6 in a book which I have edited for IFiS Publishers (Niżnik, Józef, 2006a). Some parts of Chapter 5 have been taken from my article published in the Polish Sociological Review (Niżnik, Józef, 2000). I would like to express my thanks to all the above publishers for their consent to include those fragments in the present publication.

Introduction

More and more observations of current EU political life seem to offer strong evidence that democracy has become an essential barrier to solidarity.

It is hard to find another two concepts which would be more significant in the European integration discourse than 'democracy" and "solidarity", and at the same time more ambiguous in the political practice of integration. Of course, the theoretical nature of each of these concepts is quite different. The first one has a well established theoretical background linked to its etymology while the second has been primarily a concept of everyday life and has reached its current position in the language of politics quite recently, attaining the level of a distinct chapter in the Lisbon Treaty. Both have been taken for granted as the obvious fundamental principles of this unprecedented experiment which has brought together European states despite their differences and their difficult relations in the past.

In the political language that has been developed along with European integration the concept of solidarity has been used extensively since its beginning, e.g. in the Schuman Declaration of 1950, but the variety of its meanings in different contexts has always indicated potential for confusion. At the same time the ideal of democracy has been adopted as a primary condition for any acceptable political system in Europe. Therefore, it has become one of the basic requirements within the Copenhagen criteria which must be observed by states aspiring to membership of the European Union. As it happens both concepts have signalled, above all, important values which are easier to postulate than to implement. Although no one in the EU would be ready to question the need for solidarity or the need for democracy, it is more and more clear that neither can be turned into unquestioned political practice. So, the EU has been struggling with a "democracy deficit", and the principle of solidarity has encountered a kind of "democratic barrier" in the societies of Member States. The complexity of the solidarity principle, including its instrumental value, cannot be easily grasped in the popular understanding of politics and perception of national interests which still affects the attitudes of Europeans. Therefore, domestic politics and local political interests, can by referring to democratic procedures orchestrate popular opposition against the decisions which are essential for practical demonstration of solidarity in the EU. In this way European norms, with the principle of solidarity foremost, are becoming the object of domestic power struggles.

In this book I attempt to show in more detail the context of the clash of these fundamental values which serve also as the leading political principles of European integration. Therefore several further concepts and problems are discussed, such as the issue of identity, the concept of citizenship and the problem of nationalism. Since the theoretical framework of the analysis has been organized around the idea of discourse, as an inevitable consequence some aspects of communication and the links between conceptual and normative development of the European integration must also be considered.

I hope that the analysis presented in the following chapters will be able to show both the complexity of the European process of integration and its imperative character. Within the global world there is no other future for European nations than to stay together and to do this in an ever closer union. At the same time, however, everything indicates that European precedents will allow preservation, and even increase of national and ethnic specificity. For centuries such specificity has needed guarded borders, a separate currency and military capabilities to deter neighbours' territorial ambitions. Now, despite the nationalistic appeals of some domestic politicians, it is ever more obvious to more and more people that those traditional instruments of sovereignty need to be replaced by quite opposite measures. Elimination of borders, use of a common currency and construction of common security arrangements appear to be the most rational solutions in the contemporary world in which unity does not contradict variety. Europe still seems to be on the way to proving this despite the inadequate discourse which is sometimes applied to the process of integration and may lead to a feeling of uncertainty.

Chapter I

The concept of democracy in the European integration discourse

During the 2005 international forum in Cernobbio, the Czech president, Vaclav Klaus, known for his notoriously Eurosceptical comments, suggesting a new name for the integrating Europe said: "Let us change the name: not Union any longer but Organization of the European States. I believe, the discrepancy between the real Europe and political Europe is deepening. The European Union suffers a serious democracy deficit, therefore, we had better change its aims". Reacting to Klaus's proposal, the former member of the European Commission and future Italian Prime Minister, Mario Monti responded : "I have an impression, that the citizen of the Czech Republic claims that the Union has reduced democracy. Without the Union your country would not be democratic"[1].

This episode in the constant debate over the nature of European integration seems to be very instructive for my present task. It shows, **first**, that it is possible to use the same words and operate within different discourses. **Next**, it clearly demonstrates that the concept of democracy may play an organizing role in the discourse of European integration – it certainly does in the discourse in which Vaclav Klaus has operated. And, **finally**, it makes obvious, that the discourse is not only a matter of communication but is also an important part of politics itself. In the current chapter I will attempt to develop these observations further.

Democracy became a problem in European integration as soon as this process gained a clear political dimension. Accepted in most of the world as a necessary principle and most desirable practice in the organization of political and social life, democracy has been – in a way – elevated to the position of a "political technology" of our time (Sen, Amartya, 2001). In fact "democratic" has come to mean "civilized", "acceptable", as opposed to all other "non-democratic" political regimes. This is why autocratic, even totalitarian, communist regimes pretended to be democratic, and even more, to be the only true democracies, that is, people's democracies as opposed to "bourgeois democracies".

---

1   Propozycja nowej nazwy dla Unii Europejskiej (A proposal for a new name for the EU), www.onet.pl, 4.09.2005

In this way the idea of democracy became an organizing principle in our thinking about the right political order in any plausible contemporary polity. Although the idea of democracy has been designed and practised mostly in nation-states it has been assumed that it is an obvious, primary condition also in the European Union. I will attempt to inquire whether this assumption is well-founded. The present considerations will focus on the role of language in establishing democracy in this position and on its power to steer human perception and behaviour in the area of politics and within it, of European integration.

The concept of democracy has become one of the crucial elements in theoretical reflection on politics as well as an important component of modern political discourse in general. This does not mean, however, that such a role has stimulated sufficient reflection on the part of the average users of political language. Most often, in everyday language it is just taken for granted that "democracy" belongs among the basic linguistic categories which do not require further elucidation. It is exactly the opposite situation in political science. Democracy has been established as one of the major subjects of this discipline and the enormous number of works on its problems do not help to clarify the issue but seems to make it more and more complicated (Dahl, Robert A., 1989). The works of specialists – however – who stress its "essential contestability" (Gallie, W.B., 1962), only rarely influence a popular perception of democracy understood as an idea which is basic and simple. Although the ideal of democracy serves as a core idea of a modern, western society, neither the public nor political scientists seem to notice – with very few exceptions – the special role of the concept of democracy in our political discourse. Moreover, popular evaluation of democracy continuously appears to be very ambivalent: on the one hand it has been accepted as the best form of political order, but on the other on many occasions democratic procedures are blamed for its deficiencies. In the context of European integration this ambivalence is still being deepened, and investigation of the discourse involved may allow us to see its new dimensions.

The role of discourse, its general impact on our perception of social or political reality as well as its ability to determine the significance of specific actions, depends on the "organizing units" of the discourse. The role of an "organizing unit" is usually played by one of the "main" or "key" concepts, as Michael Freeden, writing about political language, used to name them (Freeden, Michael, 1996). In fact, usually we have no doubts about which concepts in a political theory are important enough to be the "key concepts". Among them there are, for example, democracy, justice, power, liberty, and freedom. Although all such terms are usually needed in the language of political science in any theoretical or ideological orientation, which of them takes the leading role in building the sense of a theory or the sense of ideology or the sense of a mission which can be identified behind the political action is very significant. In conservative and liberal ideologies we can find very often almost the same words. The essential difference is in the "organizing units" of their discourses; the choice of those units contributes to their conservative or liberal sense, together with different assumptions and different structure of values.

The concept of democracy has slowly become – to a great extent unwilling-ly – an organizing element in the European integration discourse too. It tends to replace other concepts that earlier spontaneously aspired to such a role, like the concept of community or the concept of solidarity. It seems that the last en-largement which brought into the Union Central European post-communist countries has also had its impact on this process. After all it was on this occasion that democracy, a tacit principle of political life in Western Europe, became one of the essential conditions of the new countries' membership. Of course the issue of democracy in the EU has been discussed much earlier but it has only recently taken a central place in political debates in Europe. In a sense enlarge-ment increased awareness of a new conceptual environment that has been created by a clash of the ideal of democracy and the process of European integration. Traditional linguistic instruments, sometimes centuries old, when applied to the unprecedented political experiment (that European integration is) have made the ambivalences mentioned above especially acute. We tend to miss the fact that although we still use the well known linguistic categories like "democracy", "sovereignty", "citizenship", "state" and others, none of them has preserved its meaning unchanged. In fact each has become a part of a complete-ly new discourse, which has not necessarily been recognized sufficiently quickly as being new. As never before, social communication and the language used appeared to have direct practical and political significance. This new situation well confirms and illustrates William E. Connolly's observation that discourse "is not a prelude to politics but a dimension of politics itself" (Connolly William E., 1983:3).

In this conceptual environment European integration discourse has under-gone a reorientation which has unveiled a troublesome aspect of the issue of democracy in the European Union. Within this discourse the principle of democracy has appeared as a practically insoluble political problem: the Euro-pean Union can either save democracy by expanding its communal, federal tendencies – an option which does not receive enough public support – or maintain the present intergovernmental model of governance, which excludes any chance of a radical improvement of its present decision-making system, which does not receive public support exactly because of the democratic deficit. The network of concepts involved, many of which refer rather to the historical experiences of different nations than to the newly emerging common, supranational political entity, does not offer any coherent conceptual instruments. Analysis of the role of the concept of democracy in the European discourse may help to initiate a revision of the very principle of democracy in general or – at least – point to the need for an alternative design, organized around a different concept, of the whole European integration discourse.

In order to clarify the above thesis I will have to explain several points. First, I will clarify the concept of discourse I use and the role of specific concepts in the discourse. It appears that some concepts turn out to be organizing elements of a specific conceptual network. Next, I will discuss the relationship between discourse and political practice. Finally, I will move to issues of European integration, discussing the place of the concept of democracy in the political discourse involved.

I deliberately use the phrase "European integration discourse" instead of "discourse about the European Union" and the reasons for this should be clear after the meaning of the term has been explained. The concept of discourse has been widely used in different disciplines of social sciences and humanities in a number of meanings. In addition, there are numerous methods of discourse analysis (Van Dijk, Teun A., 1996;105). In the present study I understand discourse as a network of concepts which are semantically linked and together reflect the way in which a specific object of reflection is grasped in social communication. In most cases discourse is expressed in the form of complex linguistic messages and seems to be responsible for the general structure of sense that determines ways of apprehension of reality including its social and political dimensions. Such an approach to the role of discourse in analysis of a specific area of social life is well expressed by Ernesto Laclau, who says, that "The basic hypothesis of a discursive approach is that the very possibility of perception, thought and action depends on the structuration of a certain meaningful field, which pre-exists any factual immediacy" (Laclau, Ernesto, 1995;431). Some other authors move further, pointing to the direct impact of the language we use on social and political practice. "The language of politics is not a neutral medium that conveys ideas independently formed" – suggests William E. Connolly – "it is an institutionalised structure of meanings that channels political thought and action in certain directions" (Connolly, William E., 1983;1). This "institutionalised structure of meaning" is exactly what makes a set of concepts a discourse; an interlinked conceptual network which appears to the language users as a condition imposed on them from outside.

Michel Foucault is one of the authors whose contributions to the theory of discourse seem the most useful for our present area of study, although it is clear that some of the details of his theory go beyond my present approach. European integration offers excellent illustrations supporting some of the basic assumptions of Foucault's Archaeology of Knowledge. One of them is the problem of continuity and the lack of continuity, the problem with which Foucault starts his discussion of "the units of discourse" (Foucault, Michel, 1972;21-30). European integration is certainly a case of a break in a certain continuity; a continuity which used to be reflected by the evolution of a political form of states and relations between them. In consequence, European integration also breaks the continuity of specific political discourse, something that should be followed by a revision of our conceptual apparatus (but it is not). Also in the case of European integration discourse "we must rid ourselves of a whole mass of notions, each of which, in its own way, diversifies the theme of continuity", as Foucault put it (Foucault, Michel, 1972;21). Of course, there is a possibility to see the process of European integration differently, as a case of continuity; namely as a continuation or even development of European civilization. With such an approach also the new status of the state – to refer to Ball's illustration presented further on – may be perceived just as a stage in the development of civilization. But this will get us into debates full of further controversies concerning, for example, the concept of civilization, and the problem of inadequacy of the discourse used would only change its context.

Sometimes contemporary students of discourse try to make distinctions between different theoretical bases useful for the theory of discourse. According to Ernesto Laclau such different bases are offered by the poststructuralist theory of sign, on one side and Foucault's archaeology of knowledge, on the other. The first approach is represented by such authors as Roland Barth, Jacques Lacan and Jacques Derrida. Laclau, pointing to the same inspiration formulates the concept of discourse "as a meaningful totality, that goes beyond the distinction between linguistic and non-linguistic phenomena" (Laclau, Ernesto, 1995;435). It is clear, though, that he profits also from Foucault's inspiration and his distinction reflects only a difference of accent in these two ways of building up the concept of discourse. In fact, both these theoretical frameworks lead to an idea of discourse which is not only useful for the theory of communication but also serves certain epistemological and social functions. These are exactly the functions that are of interest to us in the present text. Therefore – unlike most of the authors who on the basis of chosen definitions and methods of discourse analysis are studying specific aspects of the political system of the EU (Diez, Thomas, 1999, 2001) – I attempt to look at the mechanisms which in social communication decide about perception of European integration. In those mechanisms a crucial role belongs to the concepts used. It appears that one of them is the concept of democracy, which indeed appears to be an organizing element in the European integration discourse.

Our object of interest in this text is European integration understood both as a process of political transformation in Europe and as the social and psychological changes caused by this process. In fact this is how European integration is usually apprehended in writings and discussions on popular perception of the European political reality. Therefore, I will take into consideration – first of all – common thinking, which is usually expressed in every day applications of political ideas in communication by members of society, but also to a great extent in the language of journalists and politicians. Theoretical reflection on European integration, including a variety of "theories of integration", in most cases appears to be a case of theorizing *ex post*, in which already accomplished integration is being analysed and explained (Hix, Simon, 1999, Niżnik, Józef, 2011a). The discourse involved is made up of many concepts which are constitutive for the political life of contemporary societies. But each of these concepts has its origins, history and its own place in social consciousness. Some of them – like the concept of power – are mostly an instrument of description, while others – like the concept of sovereignty – function in social consciousness mostly as a value; moreover as a value which is autonomous and fundamental. Although all are susceptible to a continuous evolution of their meanings, this fact in most cases escapes the attention of the average user of language who acquires these concepts in a process of socialization and accepts them as a part of reality. Such "inertia of concepts" is usually enabled by tradition, mythology and literature (Niżnik, Józef, 1979;106) . Our present area of interest is close to the field which has been called by Terence Ball "critical conceptual history" (Ball, Terence, 1988;14). However, there is at least one difference. Ball is fascinated by the relationship between the institutions of public life and the understanding of basic concepts of politics; he believes that evolution of institutions leads to changes in the meaning of given words as in his example of the institution of the state and the concept of power (Ball, Terence, 1988;82). He seems less interested in the changes of politics that are unprecedented, and so much faster that the concepts used to describe them are unable to reflect the essential difference in political reality. And this is exactly the case of European integration.

There is no doubt that also in this case the changed political reality of Europe will slowly transform the connotations of the concepts used in political language, in some cases for centuries already. But before that moment comes, both the theory and the practice of politics have to face the inertia of meanings that have been inherited from the past. So far this situation is the source of a troublesome inadequacy of European integration discourse and of the political process that goes on in integrating Europe. The problem with democracy in the EU is part of this.

Observation of the political behaviour of people who are directly embraced by European integration allows us to see that a successful process of integration requires changes that go beyond material, legal and institutional spheres. As important, if not more important from the sociological point of view, are the changes in the conceptual environment which constitutes political discourse. The significance of this environment is especially clear when taking into consideration some of the distinct features of European integration.

First, European integration is to a great extent the project of elites who have the continuous task of attracting "the masses" to their idea. Underlying this view there is the assumption that the masses have not much to say and, therefore, the whole process has failed to observe the principles of democracy. **Second,** some aspects of the process of integration have become an object of electoral rhetoric which does not care about clear language or the meanings of basic concepts. On the contrary, from the semantic point of view some concepts may be consciously used in a wrong way if such a step happens to be instrumental for political aims. Quite often politicians or journalists refer to meanings that are established in the social consciousness even if they know that those meanings are inappropriate for the description of contemporary social and political processes (Schwilk, Heimo, 1997). **Third,** many of the concepts essential in any political discourse have been created in the remote past and their present applications almost inevitably carry misunderstandings.

These three observations indicate a quite specific social dimension of European integration which links the discourse and the substance of this process; it is indeed the case of discourse which is itself politics. These observations are also most relevant when discussing the issue of democracy in the EU. Therefore I will devote now a few more words to each of them starting with the first.

Like many other theses in the area of European integration the suggestion that this process is elite-driven, and by the same token undemocratic, is also debatable. Its opponents point out that after all the whole process is under the control of democratically elected national governments (Moravcsik, Andrew, 2002). Supporters, on the other hand, stress that the very idea of democracy has been becoming increasingly an abbreviation for procedures which do not have much to do with the will of "masses". In general, however, there is no doubt that the elite/masses or elite/public division leads us directly to still more difficult aspects of democracy in the EU. In fact one can say that the idea of democracy can hardly be applied to the European Union. The problem is that all cases of democratic systems known earlier have been applied within states, and were closely linked to their systems of governance. The European Union appears to be an exceptional political entity, previously unknown. In addition to a number of other differences, it tends to assume a unifying system of governance while separate governments of the participating states are still in place. Democracy is supposed to be the core principle in both cases, but in both of them this principle seems to be questioned by the process of European integration. While the EU is accused of a democratic deficit it constantly gains more and more impact on the legal framework of Member States governed within the scheme of parliamentary democracy. The superiority of a Union law over national regulations (established by democratic procedures) in effect also limits democracy in all participating nation states.

Let us however take for granted the thesis that European integration has been so far accomplished in accordance with accepted democratic procedures. Even then the issue of the role of the political elite remains an important question. Democratic procedures mean that in societies embraced by integration there are two categories of members: (1) Those, who due to their legitimate power are in a position to create political and economic projects that determine the continuity or development of their societies, states or territorial units and (2) those, who are later subjected to those projects. Among the first group there are members of parliament, leaders of political parties, members of governments etc., in other words – the political elite. The second group is comprised by "the masses" or "the public". It is true, that decisions of the elite are based on their mandate received in democratic elections. But it is well known, that – for a variety of reasons – the opinions of European societies about important issues of European integration differ from the opinions of the political elites of those societies (Hooghe, Liesbet, 2003). The idea of citizens' engagement that makes sense of the civil society concept does not eliminate the problems that have appeared along with the elite/public distinction. There are many indications that the conception of civil society in many cases functions as a substitute for participation in decision-making. A variety of non-governmental organizations, social movements and associations offer a field for action to those who are in need of such activity, but their impact on the political decisions that are made by members of the government is in many cases illusory, or anyway very indirect. Murray Edelman formulated this in a very good way saying that, "It is therefore political actions that chiefly shape men's political wants and 'knowledge', not the other way around" (Edelman, Murray, 1985). In many cases equally illusory are the control functions of civil society since the different aims and values of different organizations effectively neutralize their real impact on political decisions.

Members of the political elite and the public have at their disposal a conceptual apparatus which may be used both for the design of political conceptions and for them to be received by the public in a process of social communication. However, such conceptual apparatuses may only appear to be the same in both instances and in reality refer to different discourses. The effectiveness of the link between civil society and "the communicative structure" of society assumed in Habermas's idea of a deliberative democracy may be very misleading (Habermas, Jürgen, 1966). All institutional innovations in the realm of politics – including the very idea of the European Union – have to be described not only in the language of international treaties but also in language that can be understood by all participants of a common discourse. Usually, when innovations come into being such language already exists. But the authors of those innovations – who, most often are the members of a political elite – consciously or unconsciously modify the meanings of traditional concepts and step by step change the whole discourse. Those changes, however, are not so obvious to the rest of society, that is to the "masses" or "public". In effect, the elite/masses divide has also been reflected in the mode of participation in a political discourse. Depending on the context, the political elite may adopt different strategies in its communication with the public: it may either attempt to disclose conceptual modifications or to camouflage them. Also, there is no lack of examples of uses of political language in which traditional meanings are alternately used with new ones, more adequate to the changed political reality, if such a practice proves to be instrumental for supporting certain arguments. Cases of such behaviour make the division mentioned above, that is the division between those who create the discourse and those who are only its users (participants), all the more evident.

Involuntarily, the whole system of education also contributes to this state of affairs. Education has to refer to certain canons of knowledge which are very resistant to change, and whose modification usually requires a long process which inevitably lags behind social or political change. Transmission and internalisation of the meanings of basic elements of political language, and in effect of a certain discourse, goes on in a continuous process of socialization. Therefore, people face political reality, including European integration, with the help of conceptual instruments created in the past for completely different theoretical and practical aims. During the centuries, with the help of those instruments, historical events important for the group have been apprehended, framing the mode of perception of significant areas of social life and a structure of values that has been transmitted from generation to generation. The current process of European integration has no reference either in individual experience or in the collective memory of the European societies. This does not mean, however, that it has not been apprehended conceptually. As Murray Edelman expresses it: "People read their own meanings into situations that are unclear or provocative of emotions" (Edelman, Murray, 1985;30). Of course, those meanings have their own genealogy and unwillingly locate new political events and institutions in the familiar contexts known from the past. Hence European integration discourse is far from being a common communication framework for all Europeans. In other words, this may be the most difficult barrier for the emergence of a European public sphere, that is of "a network for communicating information and points of view" (Habermas, Jürgen, 1966; 360). New EU citizens from Central Europe certainly have quite a different experience from those in Western Europe. Experiences of political and cultural domination and exclusion cannot leave their integration discourse intact and no doubt also contribute to the previously mentioned ambivalence when evaluating democracy. There are, however, aspects of the democratic process which are common, although far from being indisputable. Probably one of the most important is the problem of accountability.

The concept of accountability became part of the European integration discourse together with the concept of democracy, and both terms reflected some uncertainties regarding the new political system emerging in Europe. European integration, which has developed within a western world attached to the idea of democracy, should not give any reasons for doubt that the new political reality is democratic and accountable. However, this unprecedented political experiment needed new institutions and regulations as well as new forms of governance. These necessary political innovations created a new environment, earlier completely unknown to the public, and made the ideal of democracy problematic. In this new supranational context, with its mechanisms of multi-level governance, the accountability of institutions and public functionaries has become the primary concern both of the public and of political scientists (Harlow, Carol and Eawlings· Richard, 2006). At the same time, the very concept has been made an object of theoretical and empirical studies.

Probably the most intriguing feature of the concept of accountability is the uncertain relation between the theoretical and practical dimensions of this term. In most of its applications in the language of politics or political theory "accountability" appears as an obvious category, which is substantiated by its origins in accounting in the sense of a book keeping (Bovens, Marc, 2006). In fact, however, its uses both in theory and in everyday language refer to a variety of aspects of political institutions and people involved in political activity in a democratic systems. This variety somehow escapes the attention of the average users of language and of most of the actors in political life. Therefore, at least in the English language, "accountability" functions almost as a basic term. Although vocabularies of many languages are lacking words equivalent to the English "accountability", some requirements covering expectations expressed in English by this term can be found in all languages. However, a closer look at these expectations shows that "accountability" is a very complex concept which – in practice – gets "fragmented" even when the general concept exists, as is the case, for example, of the Bulgarian language. Depending on real problems and local traditions, both of which contribute to a specific context for politics, this fragmentation takes different forms. Therefore, in some contexts the predominant accent of something that may be called a "checking availability" or "checking expectation" is expressed by "transparency" while in others it may be "responsibility", "responsiveness" and many more.

What is the logical, semantic, status of "accountability"? Can we understand it as a basic requirement in order for a political system to be called "democratic"? In other words is it a kind of criterion of democracy? In fact standard definitions of democracy do not have this kind of criterion spelled out. In an extended discussion of different examples of democracy, accountability does not appear as a constitutive, "technical" category. It rather functions as a useful descriptive term and is taken for granted as a part of any democratic system (Diamond, Larry and Plattner, Marc F., 2001). For example, among the "democratic principles and practices" listed in the declaration of the Warsaw meeting of the Community of Democracies in 2000 we can read "...that the legislature be duly elected and transparent and accountable to the people" (Diamond, Larry and Plattner, Marc F., 2001; XVII). The perception of accountability as a problem that may be encountered in any democracy is a relatively new perspective which has been created by the recently developing studies of governance. This perspective has also happened to be attractive for those studying the problems of representation, of the judiciary, civil society and other aspects of contemporary democracies (Niznik, Jozef and Ryabinska, Natalya, 2007). This might mean that having accepted democracy as a leading ideal for advanced political systems, we have realized that putting this ideal into practice we encounter essential practical problems that are well expressed by the concept of accountability.

It might be useful to look into a standard general definition of the concept under discussion. Webster's II New Riverside University dictionary offers simply two meanings for the term "accountable": 1. "Required to render account: answerable", 2. "Capable of being explained" (Webster's : 1984). In fact in the language of politics accountability means exactly what has been offered in this dictionary as the first meaning, that is the requirement that the account be freely available. Of course analysis of the meanings both of "account" and its "availability" has become a task for political scientists.

In the quotation from the declaration of Community of Democracies given above we may notice that accountability and transparency have been distinguished as separate requirements. In fact, in many instances, the language of politics, and especially European integration discourse, is far from making this distinction. In most cases transparency, rule of law, responsibility and responsiveness all put together usually make up the meaning of accountability. In some specific contexts any of these terms may appear as an equivalent of the English word "accountability". In fact we can hardly imagine the requirement of accountability being fulfilled when there is no transparency or responsibility or when the rule of law is deficient. On the other hand – in a specific context – each of these terms directs our attention to the different elements of a political practice and may be useful for identifying its weakest aspects. Of course, I have in mind rather the everyday language of politicians and journalists than that of political scientists.

Conceptual analysis brings some very useful results. It emerges that the concepts that might be used as equivalents of "accountability" clearly differ in terms of their practical applicability. Some seem to indicate "passive" character-istics, while others suggest more "active" attitudes.

We might have an impression that there are methods, procedures or rules which guarantee that political acts are accountable. Accountability appears here as a requirement that may be achieved by **"passive" measures**: law and formal regulations. We may find such an assumption behind some of the uses of the concept of "rule of law" in the contexts which refer to accountability. In other contexts we may find phrasing suggesting the need for more **"active" arrange-ments**. Talking about "transparency" involves the assumption that political actors **make their activities** open for public or institutional scrutiny which usually requires more than formal regulations. Only after a closer look at the applications of those terms may we discover that semantics can be misleading.

Probably the most systematic analysis of the concept of accountability has been offered by Mark Bovens (Bovens, Mark, 2006). According to Bovens accountability is a relation between an actor and a public (forum), in which:
- the actor is obliged
- to explain and justify
- his conduct
- and the forum (public) can pose additional questions

I am not going to discuss the details of this well constructed and interesting paper but will look at some of the assumptions that were not spelled out by the author. The most important one is an assumption that an actor (individual or institution) has received their power due to the will of a public (people). This is why the actor "is obliged". What does this mean in practice? This question directs us to another more fundamental, if not pragmatic, one. What do we need accountability for? Answering this trivial question reveals some aspects of the relations between the theoretical and practical meanings of this concept as mentioned earlier.

We may offer a pragmatic answer or an answer that reaches the substance. The first one is – in fact – cynical. The latter is theoretical and – it seems – idealistic, because in many cases it may appear that the postulated accountability is just an ideal which will be never achieved in practice.

The pragmatic answer would be: we need accountability to satisfy the public. The tacit belief included in this kind of answer is that the public will be satisfied by just having this opportunity which will be very rarely used. In fact, low turnouts in parliamentary elections in many democratic countries seem to support this belief. We may also notice that satisfaction arising from the level of accountability does not necessarily require respect for norms, procedures or – in general – for democracy. One might attempt to show that the populism which troubles contemporary democracy on many continents is based on this kind of relation between expectations for accountability and its empirical forms.

There is, however, a different answer to the question which indeed refers to the substance. It says: we need accountability to verify democracy. Again, the simplest example of this function of accountability is electoral democracy. If elected representatives fail to keep the promises of their election campaigns they are turned out at the next elections. We all know, though, that reality is more complicated and that different institutions and levels of governance that should be accountable are simply well insulated from this kind of verification. But still, such an understanding of accountability offers – at least in theory – the possibility of verifying also the procedures and norms that regulate the everyday practice of democracy. Of course, this "repair mechanism", which is somehow expected as a practical effect of accountability, usually becomes part of the rivalry between political parties or individual politicians, and is broadly exploited by the media which effectively influence its outcome.

What exactly, then, should we study when we decide to study political accountability? There are variety of possibilities and all seem to be relevant. Among them we can certainly list the following:

* The legal framework and its institutions, including norms and procedures. The accountability of courts according to Mortin Kinander would certainly fit into this category (Kinander, Morten, 2005).
* The functioning of political representation in a parliamentary democracy.
* Social psychological factors involved in actor-public relations.
* Communication involved in a democratic system including the role of media (Douglas, Arnold R.; 2004).
* The political awareness and political knowledge of the public which is best expressed in the idea and practice of civil society.

The crucial question that we still have to answer is why accountability should become a topic for research, something which certainly indicates that there is a "problem of accountability", that there is a demand to conform to this requirement formulated even in societies commonly accepted as democratic. It seems that the problem of accountability suggests some kind of deficiency of democracy (a threat to its principles) or/and difficulties in maintaining its crucial benefits. Democracy appears to be a system which does not rely on trust but demands instruments for constant checking. From this point of view accountability deserves attention no matter how perfect democracy is in a specific country. Therefore, it certainly needs to be studied in a system in which democracy is under debate, and – moreover – in a system which is accused of having a "democracy deficit". This is exactly why accountability has become such an important element of contemporary political discourse and a topic so intensely discussed among the theorists of European integration (Mark Bovens, Deidre Curtin and Paul 't Hart, 2010). Moreover, everything indicates that the outcome of this discussion may affect the future of the European Union. The most recent developments in European integration, including the failure of ratification of the Constitutional Treaty in two core countries of the EU, show that the problem of accountability cannot be limited to academic discussions.

Also, the study of accountability must go beyond research into its institutional or legal aspects and include analysis of a common discourse, and of the public understanding of democracy. In other words: the problem is not just "accountability" understood as a theoretical concept but also as the ways people use it when expressing their expectations regarding democracy. Analysing social perception of European integration one cannot overestimate the significance of reflection devoted to discourse. Laclau points out accurately, that " there is a proliferation of 'floating signifiers' in society, and political competition can be seen as attempts by rival political forces to partially fix those signifiers to particular signifying configurations. Discursive struggles about the ways of fixing the meaning of a signifier like 'democracy', for instance, are central to explaining the political semantics of our contemporary political world"(Laclau, Ernesto, 1995;435). Therefore, the significance of studies of European integration discourse becomes especially evident when its crucial concepts are made the subject of such studies. I am talking about the concepts organizing the whole discourse, about those which determine the very nature of formulated messages and the conceptions involved. Consent to changes in social and political reality, or its absence, depends greatly on the understanding of such conceptions. There is no doubt that the concept of democracy is one of them.

Reflection on the European integration discourse urges us to ask whether the concept of democracy is indeed the one that we should necessarily refer to when discussing fundamental issues of European integration. I believe it is not, and that putting "democracy" in the centre of the European debate makes us blind to the specificity of the whole process of European integration. We need to organize European integration discourse around other concepts that are able to stimulate public support for necessary institutional reforms of the Union. For instance such concepts as "solidarity" or "security". Of course, "democracy" would remain a part of this discourse, slowly gaining an adequate meaning which would make any complaints about a democracy deficit unsubstantiated.

Chapter II

European integration and the concept of solidarity

The current chapter is devoted to the concept of solidarity and its role in the European integration discourse. The concept of solidarity – applied to relations among European states – made an appearance already in the Schuman Declaration in which it served as one of the organizing elements of the discourse constituted by this declaration. "Solidarity" has remained an important term in the description of the aims of European integration since then, but its meaning has been changing over time depending on the context. Solidarity of states may imply the responsibility of each state for the security of other states or for their well-being; well-being may refer to the standard of living or to the quality of the natural environment or even to the satisfaction of people with the domestic politics of their nation-state. The last example might be somehow confusing, though.

Currently the term "solidarity" has ceased to be one of those crucial elements that serve as organizing units of the discourse, and it has been replaced in this role by other terms; most recently by the concept of democracy. I am trying to characterize the nature of the tension between those two ideas – solidarity and democracy – and to explain the reasons which led to their clash. Referring to the most recent changes in the European integration discourse, and the re-appearance of "solidarity" in the new context, I will attempt to reconstruct the current meanings of the concept of solidarity in order to estimate its potential which could be instrumental for the needed reorientation of the European integration process. Finally, I will try to look at the impact of the idea of a welfare state on the development of the EU social policy.

The concept of solidarity has been for a long time one of the most useful linguistic instruments which was spontaneously expected to oppose particularism or rivalry as well as the fight for dominance, and imply cooperation for the common good. Sometimes it even indicates an important moral imperative. Most recently solidarity has appeared to be a very relevant issue when discussing the moral basis for the idea of a welfare state (Ferrera, Maurizio 2005, Arts, Wil and Gelissen, John 2001, Schuyt, Kees 1998) or when looking for the foundations of social cohesion often identified as "social solidarity" (Widegren, Örjan 1997). Kees Schuyt, putting solidarity foremost among the three main principles of a welfare state understands it simply as a norm which requires that "nobody should drop below the level necessary for a decent existence in a free society" (Schuyt, Kees 1998;298). Moreover, when looking for normative significance of the idea of community –an idea after all well established as one of the main categories of sociology – some authors quite correctly turn their interest toward the concept of solidarity (Mason, Andrew 2004) .

"Solidarity" used to appear as well in everyday language to signify an important social attitude, emotional engagement or objective of social action, as in different disciplines of social sciences where – beginning with the thought of E. Durkheim – it served specific theoretical functions. The relation between theorizing in social sciences and everyday thinking appears here quite relevant to the present analysis. Since social sciences, including political science, usually directly refer to social or political reality many of their technical terms have appeared useful in the language of practice. In this way some of the conceptual tools of those disciplines which earlier had been borrowed from everyday language are returning to common language but substantially changed and endowed with normative or ideological significance. There is no doubt that the concept of solidarity is a perfect example of such a term.

Any attempt to classify different meanings of solidarity will be probably far from perfect. For the current analysis I would like to concentrate on the functions of this concept and distinguish the following functions depending on two different points of view:

• from the **point of view of motivation** (which can be identified behind its use): instrumental and normative functions,

• from the **point of view of its pragmatic value:** descriptive function which can serve either theoretical or rhetorical aims.

These functions of the concept of solidarity can be easily seen in the practical applications of European integration discourse. However, the context which is of interest to us here appears quite complicated because European integration is a multidimensional process. It is certainly an important feature of the European economy but its political or social aspects are, no doubt, of a paramount importance. The concept of solidarity in the European integration discourse may refer to any of those aspects although in each of them it can have different meanings. On the other hand in all of its applications there must be something that justifies the use of the same term which clearly adds an important component to the very meaning of European integration, no matter which aspect of the process is under consideration. Also, we should remember that the specificity of different forms of European integration discourse is determined by some of the key terms used in this conceptual network (the terms which function as "organizing units" of the discourse), and those different forms of discourse usually express different visions of an integrating Europe. Therefore, the use of the concept of solidarity in a particular meaning may directly indicate a specific vision of Europe.

Let me start then with a brief comment referring to the notion of discourse explained in the earlier chapter. Our spontaneous, "natural" attitude towards the world resembles epistemological realism; we tend to assume that reality is something "out there" which can be correctly perceived by our sensual apparatus. Only a more reflexive approach is able to bring to our attention the whole complexity of the process of cognition. For example the fact that what we perceive as "reality" is usually one of many possible aspects of our object of perception and that, depending on our ability to see different aspects, our world can at different moments appear quite different (Wittgenstein, Ludwig 1997). When discussing European integration discourse we are focusing on the network of concepts which build up a specific perspective for our human matters in the social or political realm. The discourse which is of our interest here refers to an especially complex area because it is addressing a social reality which – from the epistemological point of view – is still more problematic; we are talking about grasping the social world while being part of it.

Within such an approach the task of language goes well beyond its role as instrument of communication; language also determines our perception and actions.

"Solidarity" has not always appeared as one of the key concepts. According to Steinar Stjernø three main currents of thought have developed specific approaches to solidarity : the Marxist, social democratic and Christian democratic currents. Those "three traditions of solidarity", as Stjernø calls them, have built up different discourses of solidarity although the term itself has not necessarily appeared in the political parties' programmes. In fact, there were many cases of political language aimed at actual solidarity while giving up the term itself. For instance, quite characteristic for the origins of the welfare state was the absence from the political language used of both the concept of solidarity and the concept of the welfare state (Stjernø, Steinar 2005; 180). One could speculate that those concepts were the tacit organizing units of discourse; that they belonged to the intentions, but were not necessarily spelled out. Another way to grasp such cases would lead to the distinction between unnamed "substantive" solidarity, intentional or actual, and "ideological" solidarity, which is expressed in the language used and indicates specific ideals or even objectives in the social realm, but may be completely absent from concrete decisions and behaviour. The world communist movement, controlled and directed by the Soviet Union was a perfect example of such a situation up to the point where in

Poland in 1976 a Committee for the Defence of Workers, created by dissidents, openly opposed the policies of the Polish United Workers Party which claimed to represent the interests of all workers. In a way the concept of "solidarity" played a similar role in the 2005 presidential campaign of the late president of Poland, Lech Kaczyński, who pretended to defend solidarity supposedly endangered by the liberal orientation of his competitor. In the Polish context the use of this concept led directly to the national experience of the Solidarity Movement in 1980, although the meanings of "solidarity" in the latter case had very little in common with the meaning intended in the campaign[2].

Describing the transition from the Marxist concept of solidarity to a social democratic one Stjernø shows that it was a move from an instrumental towards normative meaning of solidarity, although this distinction has not appeared in his text: "The foundation is not seen as interests, but as ethics, humanism, empathy and compassion. The goal of solidarity is not socialism, but the creation of a feeling of community, social integration and sharing of risks" (Stjernø, Steinar, 2005; 199).

It is important to notice that both in everyday language and in specialized use in social sciences the meaning of the term "solidarity" is always dependent on the context. Its contextual character contributes to its confusing nature. Therefore, "solidarity" in sociological theory reflects a different phenomenon than in political science. Also, solidarity in political matters indicates a different aspect of collective attitudes and sentiments than in social matters. It is easy to imagine that – depending on the context – this word may be used to name quite different if not antagonistic attitudes or patterns of behaviour. For example, the solidarity of a criminal gang exactly opposes the idea of solidarity within society as a whole. However, this does not mean that the essential meaning of this concept has no common social-psychological features.

Let me then examine briefly this social-psychological core of the concept of solidarity and the attitude most often so named. In this sense, solidarity means – first – the feeling of unity of a certain group. Then, it implies the feeling of responsibility of each member of the group for the well-being of the group. Also, it indicates the readiness of the members to give up some of their autonomy for the sake of the well-being of the whole, which means that the interest of the group has been put above the interest of the individual members. Therefore,

---

2   In 1980 the Polish movement which adopted the name of Solidarity had intended, at the start, to unite the nation's opinion against communist repressions but soon it turned into a demonstration of the actual solidarity of most Poles who were ready to actively support demands formulated by the Gdansk shipyard workers, expanding later into the demands for general democratic freedom which initiated the fall of communism in Europe.

we can probably agree that solidarity is a kind of a "social feeling" understood as a sentiment of an individual which is addressed to the specific collective. This is why so often the concept of altruism appears together with the concept of solidarity and their distinction needs some theoretical work (Arnsperger, Christian and Varoufakis, Yanis 2003, Widegren, Örjan 1997;763). It is important to notice that, although in some cases the conditions for solidarity are created by interpersonal relations, this is not a precondition for this kind of attitude. After all the word "solidarity" also appeared when in response to the 2010 earthquakes which hit Haiti and then Chile people around the world spontaneously offered material or at least symbolic help as well as compassion to those affected by the disaster. It is exactly the specific discourse activated at such moments which allows us to see that the feeling of the unity of humankind may be a real experience.

It is the context which determines what kind of "group" is the object of this unique social feeling and what kind of "individual" is involved. Recalling the variety of applications of this word we know that the "group" can be a collective of people or organizations or states or even the totality of humankind. In the same way the "individual" can be a person but also an organization or the state. However, no matter what kind of entity is indicated as a group or as an individual almost in every instance the experience and the effects of solidarity reach, directly or indirectly, human individuals. The instruments that are used for this can be the policy of a state, the rules imposed by an organization, the norms established in a group of people or simply a shared feeling of compassion.

In most general terms solidarity appears to be an indispensable condition for any group to be anything more than a collection of individuals. This was exactly the observation of Durkheim when he defined the idea of a social group. The work of Steinar Stjernø, analysing the idea of solidarity in social theory, socialist movements and religions appears to be just a study in the history of ideas, with clear focus on the impact which the concept of solidarity had on understanding of society. "Solidarity" simply indicated the tendency to put the collective aspect of the human world over the role of the individual, something demonstrated especially in the sphere of norms.

As suggested earlier, reflection devoted to the concept of solidarity should take into consideration descriptive (serving theoretical or rhetorical aims), instrumental and normative approaches to solidarity.

In the case of a **descriptive** approach to solidarity we are mostly interested in a specific setting, social or political, which promotes certain kinds of social policy which need to be described. It might be created by the very nature of the situation or, simply, be a way in which a particular situation has been characterized without formulation of the question "why" it is like that. Pointing to solidarity usually means that we want to profit from the positive connotations which this term has. At the same time, however, using the term "solidarity" in a descriptive sense may indicate a substantial level of arbitrariness in understanding its social parameters and usually leaves all the questions about the nature or the motives for solidarity beyond our attention. Of course, this does not mean that there are cases where there are no reasons for solidarity as a form of a "social feeling" or no motives for specific behaviour which we usually associate with solidarity. In fact, in most cases behind the descriptive use of this term we may find assumptions indicating its instrumental or normative character.

The **instrumental** approach by and large stresses the common interest as the reason for solidarity, while the **normative** approach points out that demonstrating solidarity is simply right, morally correct. Spontaneous compassion for those suddenly in trouble, involving the emotional reactions of people who are strangers to each other, somehow escapes this distinction although it is also often called solidarity. My suggestion, though, would be to use other words in such cases, for example, compassion or empathy. There is no doubt, however, that any form of solidarity, whether instrumental or normative can be made more effective if supported by such emotions as compassion. Also, it is quite clear that every case of instrumental solidarity has a better chance of practical realization if supported by normative justification. Unfortunately, in most instances what is needed in order to initiate instrumental solidarity is simply knowledge, reasoning and correct definition of the situation, which are generally very difficult to achieve in the context of political struggles. This is exactly the case of the ideal of solidarity in European integration. European integration offers an exceptional example both of the power of discourse and of its complexity. The concept of solidarity has already been used extensively for a long time but on many occasions its aims were mostly **rhetorical**. It was simply assumed, that "solidarity" would bring positive moral connotations to justify particular political decisions or add such connotations to the very process of integration.

The initial reasons for solidarity, at least those spelled out in the Schumann Declaration of May 9, 1950, were instrumental. The Declaration, however, was presented at a moment in history which could easily underline its normative sense. In Schumann's text there is a clear attempt to go beyond the instrumental or merely rhetorical role of "solidarity". The document stresses a "*de facto* solidarity*" which can mean both solidarity demonstrated empirically and solidarity supported by a moral imperative. The very construction of the Schumann Declaration leaves no doubt that the concept of solidarity was an organizing unit of the discourse which was founded by this document. With the further

development of European integration, solidarity, initially understood instrumen
tally as a principle in international relations in Europe, achieved additional
significance reaching relations between the nations involved. This was quite a
natural development because such a course had been implied by the discourse
used and supported by a deliberately designed policy, beginning with the
cohesion policy already initiated by the Treaty of Rome in 1957. Cohesion
policy needed a normative background which, indeed, appeared – as European
integration was extended to include the poorer states of Southern Europe – and
then was used to justify the increase of its funding.

Although the concept of solidarity is constantly in use in the European integration discourse, at a certain point it lost its position as an organizing unit of
this discourse. This happened not because solidarity lost its moral power or
instrumental effectiveness. The reason was a general reshuffling within the
network of concepts which had composed the general structure of the European
integration discourse, due to the radical changes which occurred in Europe with
the end of communism, and in European Community with the foundation of the
European Union. Both facts brought the concept of democracy to public awareness and to the centre of political discourse.

Unexpectedly the issue of democracy – so far taken for granted as an obvious feature of the integrating Europe – became a problem. The Treaty on the EU
brought the issue to the attention of people and among them, of political scientists. The problem of the democracy deficit suddenly displaced permissive
consensus and European political elites' management of European integration
started to be questioned. Also, with rapid enlargement of the EU the lack of
popular support for the financial instruments of cohesion policy in the countries
which are "net contributors" became a problem which hit one of the crucial
mechanisms of integration. The problems with multiculturalism, experienced in
some member states, added new fears which were clearly very dysfunctional for
the progress of solidarity (Amin Ash, 2004). All these developments created
conditions for Eurosceptical arguments which immediately became useful in
political struggles for power in most of the EU states. The crucial value needed
in such a situation was democracy, and its role has been greatly increased by the
fall of communism in Europe. Steinar Stjernø quite correctly noticed that "the
meaning of solidarity changes not only according to how the different aspects of
solidarity are combined, but also through the different meanings of these other
key concepts, and how these are related to the different meanings of the concept
of solidarity" (Stjernø Steinar, 2005;.245).

In fact, the problem with the concept of solidarity was not its meaning but
its role in the discourse. As a result of the changes mentioned, "democracy"
became the organizing unit in the European integration discourse, reorienting

the whole discourse and, later on, the whole process of European integration. Of course, "solidarity" remained among the most important concepts of this discourse but its role appears to be mostly rhetorical. In public debates in many EU Member States European matters have been more and more often used by domestic politicians to justify unpopular decisions. The discourse developed around the concept of "democracy" rather than "solidarity" appeared to be safer and more effective in dealing with such dilemmas as social security versus economic effectiveness or national unity versus European integration. Since the ideal of democracy has been established as a leading political value which does not need any justification, all other values, including solidarity, have been placed under its reign. It was in this situation that in 2005 ratification of the Constitutional Treaty failed in two founding members of the European Communities.

As a result of such reorientation of discourse, the European Union is facing problems with decision making in strategic areas concerning, for example, further development of its cohesion policy or EU enlargement.

Political leaders of all Member States are increasingly aware of European structural problems, e.g. its ageing population, as well as difficulties in the world economic situation and the impact of those factors on the future of the so called "European social model" which, in fact, is another name for the idea of the welfare state. However, in popular understanding, openly supported by populist politicians in some EU countries, the welfare state is threatened by supposedly excessive contributions to the EU budget and cheap labour available in the poorer new Member States. In this way in the course of European integration the principle of solidarity clashes with the principle democracy. At the same time the normative power of the welfare state, supposed to fight the structural conditions for exclusion, seems to weaken too. Writing about the prospects for post-industrial solidarity, already 10 years ago John Andersen suggested the need for an instrumental approach to solidarity writing that "we must emphasize the dysfunctionality of exclusion and discuss the positive functions of inclusion" (Andersen John, 1999;384). Andersen has perceived "post-industrial meritocratism" as the reason for the failure of the politics of inclusion. Although I do not share his view on the role of meritocratic social stratification I tend to agree with his instrumental approach to solidarity. Both in the domestic policies of the Member States and in the EU strategy for progress, solidarity, in all the variety of its meanings, seems to be beneficial as much for the Member States as for the EU. And satisfaction from doing "the right things" may in the future become an additional social achievement of the EU.

Since the concept of solidarity has been linked to the idea of a welfare state and both imply social policy I would like now to devote a few pages to the impact of the idea of a welfare state on the possibility of developing an EU social policy.

The idea of a welfare state, as well as the variety of its implementations in different European states, has made the development of an EU social policy an exceptionally difficult task. In order to overcome the rules adopted in the EU of division of competences, which earlier left social policy within the competence of Member States, several inventions have appeared. Among them are the Open Method of Coordination and the Charter of Fundamental Rights of the European Union. Nevertheless the crucial concept which still works as a mind-set in this area is that of a welfare state. Since in different Member States the understanding of it varies, the development of an EU social policy will depend on several conditions. The most important seem to be the following two.

First, the progress of community method-based governance of the EU, which would limit its intergovernmental dimension. **Second**, the innovative coexistence of a principle of state social protection with competitiveness of the EU on the global scene.

Both conditions are linked to the necessary revision of the understanding of social protection which, in the general perception, has been tied to the idea of a welfare state. In its current role this idea works as a barrier to a realistic and effective social policy. In addition, some of the current instruments of social policy which are in place in different EU member states need to be revised. Such revision appears almost impossible if left entirely within the competence of the Member States. Therefore the primary condition of the future social policy of the EU is a radical strengthening of community method-based governance of the EU. In order to make it feasible some measures that would increase EU solidarity seem to be imperative.

It is increasingly obvious, that almost all major problems of the EU have links to the inefficiency of governance of the Union, which is the result of its ambiguous, "hybrid" political form. In fact the essence of the problem lies in the fact that the EU is still far from being a real union. The disaster in the global financial system, which also revealed the weaknesses of the fiscal regime of the Eurozone, made it clear that further development of the EU and even its sustainability will be impossible without greater financial discipline within the whole community. The social unrest in Greece, following announcement of the government's budgetary austerity measures, imposed by international institutions in order to tighten the country's spending and enforce a rigid saving policy, was a spectacular demonstration of the linkages between fiscal and social policy. The dissatisfaction of the public in reaction to similar measures in other EU states, for example in Spain but also in the UK, showed that common EU rules, both in financial and social policies, might have spared the EU at least some of the effects of the economic and financial crises. The problem is that both areas –fiscal and social – have been left within the Member States' competences. The EU Stability and Growth Pact was limited to the outcome of the internal fiscal policy and its macroeconomic indicators, which, as it happened, was not enough. Only after the dramatic development of the situation in Greece did it become clear that what the EU needs is deeper intervention by supranational EU authorities in economic and financial policies as well as in the practices of the Member States' governments. The possibility of such intervention will have to be based on legal solutions which must be established through the revision of the existing treaty.

In such improvements to the EU mechanisms of governance, social policy is becoming the natural next target. However, in this area Europeanisation may lead to a conflict between the ideal of solidarity – which is supposed to serve the unity of the Union – and the different approaches of the Member States to social policy. Maurizio Ferrera put this in compact form saying that "integration has launched a direct challenge to the *boundaries* of welfare, *qua* institutional foundations of its solidaristic mission." (Ferrera, 2005;11) The main problem is that in order to justify solidarity within the EU, the basic norms of social policy of all countries should be very similar if not identical. The reality is far from that, making the principle of solidarity controversial. How can the government of the country with a retirement age of 65 explain to its citizens that it should help to pay the bills of another EU state in which the retirement age is e.g. 60?

In the background of the whole dilemma one can find the idea of the welfare state, which has become a framework for thinking about the relations between the state and citizens as far as their well-being is concerned. Since it is the state's practical implementation of this idea which is furnishing it with meaning in everyday discourse, the idea of a welfare state is just taken for granted, and for the average citizen its sense very rarely becomes a matter for reflection. Moreover, it is inevitably tied to the institution of a nation state (Martinsen, 2005). Therefore, transnationalisation of welfare seems to be the essential change in the popular mindset needed as soon as the concept of an EU social policy appeared. This is how in the European framework the welfare state has turned into a "social Europe" or the "European social model". Of course, the variety of understandings of "social Europe" in different European countries reflects the variety of meanings which the idea of a welfare state has in those countries (Cousins, 2005, Kvist and Saari, 2007). Therefore, some authors put it directly: "Contrary to official European policy discourse, there are not one but many European social models" (Hermann and Hofbauer, 2007; 131). The concept of a "European social model", which initially was to differentiate the economic and social strategies of the European Community and the US, became a kind of promise of Europeanisation of social policies of the EU Member States. Since it has remained quite vague it has been adopted by a variety of political orientations serving different political and ideological objectives. Also, its vagueness has allowed many redefinitions of this concept, although initially (something that has been attributed to J. Delors), it had a clearly socialist appeal. So it is no surprise that left-oriented groups are using it as a synonym for a socialist vision of the European Union (Hermann and Hofbauer, 2007).

In fact, the whole problem appears to be – first of all – a problem of discourse. The use of the same words, that is "welfare state" and "social Europe", creates an impression that the users are operating within the same discourse while, in reality, the normative framework of "social Europe", which can be reconstructed from the European Union's regulations, is usually quite far from its national interpretations in specific Member States. One can only sense that the mental association of welfare with the nation state inevitably had to clash with attempts by the supranational system of the EU to get involved in social policy despite the lack of necessary competences. The introduction to the White Paper on the European Social Policy, published by the European Commission in 1994, received the title: "Preserving and Developing the European Social Model". It starts with a section on shared values that included "democracy and individual rights, free collective bargaining, the market economy, equality of opportunity for all and social welfare and solidarity" (p.2). This list of values says a lot about the approach to social policy which has been demonstrated in the White Paper. According to this document the European Social Model cannot be limited to narrowly understood social protection but must include basic economic and political mechanisms which create the necessary conditions for social policy. Although employment, competitiveness and convergence were the main issues among the social objectives of the Union addressed in the text, one has a feeling that the focus of this publication was on the general economic and political framework of the newly created European Union. Therefore, by presenting a view on employment and labour relations the White Paper underlined their role for the competitiveness of the Union. In addition, direct reference to the idea of a welfare state was made in the section entitled: "Maintaining and adapting the European model of the welfare state" (p.35). This title is especially instructive since it includes both the intention of maintaining the welfare state and its "adaptation", which indicates that in the European framework the very idea of a welfare state needs some kind of rearrangement. The view presented in this section recognises "the diversity of social protection systems" but at the same time stresses that "Member States have agreed to foster the convergence of their social protection policies", and this observation is followed with a few recommendations which were general enough not to violate

Member States' authority in the area. The 14 years that followed proved both the attachment of Member States to their specific understandings of the idea of the welfare state and the unchanged view on the essential values of the European Social Model (What is European Social Model?, 2008). It was, and still is, a period of struggle aimed at taking responsibility for social matters in the EU, while citizens (*qua* national politicians) were still not ready to grant the EU the necessary competences. The Lisbon Treaty, in Article 2C of its Horizontal Amendments, puts social policy, among the competences which the Union shares with the Member States in some aspects ("for the aspects defined in this Treaty"). Nevertheless the crucial concept which still works as a mind-set in this area is that of a welfare state.

Gráinne de Búrca points out that there is no agreement on the essential question, that is whether EU welfare policy is desirable at all (Búrca, 2005-2). In this situation it is justified to ask whether European social policy does indeed exist, and how it is possible. Its presence in official documents of the EU, and observation of some of the internal regulations in the Member States led several authors to the conclusion that what we observe is a Europeanisation of social protection which itself is secured by the Member States (Kvist and Saari, 2007; 1). This handy concept, Europeanisation, refers to the impact of EU soft law on social policies of the Member States. After all, the EU in its present political form lacks the basic instruments for enforcing any such policy, starting with the lack of a separate social policy budget which could be supported by the European tax system. Maurizio Ferrera, writing about this issue, nevertheless suggests that the EU has developed "a distinctive social policy, essentially of a regulatory type" (Ferrera, 2005; 36). Such observations basically cover what other authors have in mind when talking about the mechanism of Europeanisation. It is clear that the ongoing process of integration, involving free movement of people, required regulations in this area. They appear e.g. already in the Treaty of Amsterdam in its Social Protocol, and then in different Directives and Regulations. The aim of this process was to enforce certain principles in social protection, which it is expected will be fulfilled by the Member States, no matter where their nationals who are to profit from these principles reside. Slowly, certain social benefits secured by social security schemes in the Member States have been granted to all residents, no matter what their nationality, as long as they are EU citizens (with exceptions, which have included also some third country nationals of a special status, for example refugees). Dorte Sindbjerg Martinsen discussed the issue in the framework of exportability and deterritorialization of welfare (Martinsen, 2005).

The process of Europeanisation of social protection has been perceived also as a process of convergence of the social policies of the EU Member

States although the progress of this convergence is still quite modest (Camina da, Goudswaard, Van Vliet, 2010). Effective convergence would require elimination of diversities which still exist in the understanding of what the welfare state is supposed to be responsible for. At the core of the debate, we can always find the idea of the welfare state, since no matter what the Member States' instruments of social protection are they are presumed to be the implementation of norms which are implied by this idea in a particular society. According to some participants in these debates it is the welfare state idea which needs reform. Maurizio Ferrera and Martin Rhodes formulated this suggestion in the following words: "The European welfare state is now faced with a difficult challenge of internal restructuring, involving a 'recasting' of many of its traditional instruments and objectives. But what exactly is the nature of this challenge? What specific features of social protection 'European style' are most in need of adoption?"(Ferrera, Rhodes,2002;1). According to these authors the main challenges are internal and socioeconomic in nature and include demographic change, rising costs of health care, high unemployment, low economic growth, and also new patterns of social life affecting households and family relationships. It is clear that the background of those challenges may differ in particular states. Therefore, the measures needed to face them would be also different. Nevertheless one can expect that certain norms of social protection as well as level of support could be comparable within the entire Union. Moreover, the welfare state idea has to face challenges which, at least in part, have originated in Europe with the process of integration (Bommes and Geddes, 2000, Cousins, 2005). According to Fritz Scharpf European integration brought a "constitutional asymmetry" between economic policy, stressing market efficiency, and social policy, focusing on social protection (Scharpf, 2002).

Although most of the publications discussed so far were written before the 2004 enlargement, they all indicate an important problem: the ambivalence between the need for EU engagement in social protection and its constitutional weakness in this area. In the absence of constitutional solutions, rescue has been offered by organizational and legal "inventions", such as the Open Method of Coordination and the Charter of Fundamental Rights. Both inventions were aimed at avoiding existing barriers to common policies in certain areas including social policy.

It looks as if the development of EU governance proceeds through measures which conceal their community method-based approach and pretend to develop further intergovernmental decision making. The Lisbon Treaty after all has been publicized as a step towards strengthening the intergovernmental dimension of the EU political system. Europe seems to be in a period in which some of the national elites have decided to stress particularistic local interests rather than European ones. This may suggest that in the current situation, with its revival of nationalistic sentiments, development of Eurosceptic attitudes, and problems with the unity of the Eurozone, there is little chance for an open strategy of deepening European integration by moving towards stronger political union. On the other hand such vital matters as financial stability, security and the need for competitiveness in an ever more aggressive global context will probably leave no alternative to stronger political unity of the EU. The debates about solutions for the fiscal problems of European countries showed the radical change of attitudes of many European leaders toward this option. The next necessary step will be to gain public support for this course of development. EU social policy may in this way become a very important issue although, for the reasons explained earlier, not an easy one.

Europeanisation of social protection appears to be a complicated task exactly because it involves a "recasting" of the European welfare state idea (Ferrera and Rodes, 2002, Greve, 2003-2) . Bent Greve, however, offers a solution which is supposed to allow both convergence of the European models of a welfare state and preservation of some national specificities. According to Greve the move toward the common European model does not exclude differences in priorities in different countries: "The overall convergence towards a common level of spending and ways of financing can thus function well together with a respect for difference in prioritizing different areas. Politics thus matter but more as a way of making priorities between different choices than having an impact on the overall level" (Greve, 2003; 558).

The general impression from the views reported earlier is that Europeanization of social policy can be perceived either as a move toward a common European model of the welfare state or as a convergence of social protection schemes existing in the Member States. The difference seems to be only one of the language adopted since successful convergence would mean that the existing models of the welfare state would become very similar and, in effect, would accomplish the idea of a social Europe . However, if the suggestion of Greve were to be implemented this would be a social Europe with diversified priorities in particular states. This is why it might be useful to look at the most general elements of the idea of a welfare state which cannot be abandoned when moving to the concept of "social Europe". I have in mind exactly those elements which currently lead to differences between the Member States. These differences depend on the internal regulations which turn the idea of a welfare state into specific norms of social policy. What, then, are the necessary elements of the idea of a welfare state? It seems that this idea implies the following general regulations:

a)   a scheme of redistribution of wealth,
b)   a recognition of the responsibility of a state for the welfare of people,
c)   specified rights of citizens,
d)   the norms of inclusion and exclusion which regulate who in a particular society is entitled to what.

In fact the ideas of social Europe and the welfare state contain the same elements. Also, those concepts are just a framework for a policy, and not the policy itself. All controversies and differences in social policies between Member States have been caused by the details of regulations such as the level of taxation, the level of the minimum wage, the rules for granting unemployment benefits and the duration and level of payments, the retirement pension system, health services, the insurance system and so on. Economic disparities between the Member States would continue to affect such regulations. How far and on what basis can the European Union intervene in order to guarantee that they still remain within "European social model"? This is exactly where the Open Method of Coordination proves to be helpful (Heidenreich and Zeitlin, 2009). It is interesting how OMC has become a substitute for an institution. After all, at its starting point it accepts an existing legal situation which does not allow direct intervention by the Union in social matters unless human rights are violated. The essence of the procedure is a kind of proposal which cannot be refused. It is called a "method", it appeals for "coordination" and it is "open". OMC is just a way to engage Member States in common efforts toward common objectives, standards and practices which can be achieved thanks to organized mutual learning. It is expected that in this way this procedure, although slow, will bring the EU to the common welfare regime that would make Europe a "social Europe".

The question is whether OMC, with all its ingenuity, is enough to make effective social policy of the EU a reality, whether the substitute can be adequate as a measure to take the place of an institutional solution. It looks as if what need to be "europeanised" are exactly the details of social policy that most Member States want to keep among their competences. How to move forward in this situation? The answer to this question concludes the present chapter.

The development of the EU social policy is closely linked to the development of its governance system and political form. The current inefficiency of its social policy can be attributed to the present division of competences according to which the decisive role belongs to the Member States' governments. National politicians, in their struggle for power, are profiting from the overwhelming belief of their electorates in the role of the nation state in taking responsibility for their welfare. In effect, the idea of a welfare state works as a barrier to the development of the EU social policy which lacks the necessary instruments. There is a still more serious consequence of this situation. The domestic politics of the Member States are predominantly centred on local matters while the success of the EU (and in effect of its Member States) depends on taking into consideration the competitiveness of the Union's economy on the global scene. Since an adequate social policy is supposed to serve greater cohesion of the EU and improve the effectiveness of labour, imposition in this area of a common normative framework would be beneficial for the global position of the EU economy. Of course, such a normative framework can still respect some national specificities, for example in the prioritization of social objectives as Bent Greve suggested.

In order to achieve this situation the European Union needs to increase its political integration. The idea of the welfare state can be turned into common European norms of social policy only by moving some decision making in this area from the nation state to the supranational organs of the EU. Common EU norms in social matters can in the Member States result in comparable instruments of social policy, for example in the rules setting retirement and unemployment benefits. Such comparability – along with EU fiscal discipline – is imperative if solidarity is to be the leading principle in the Union.

Therefore, the EU needs deeper political integration allowing more competences for its supranational organs as well as its most democratic institution, the European Parliament . At the same time, the intergovernmental position of the European Council could be counterbalanced by introducing a direct, common election of the President of this institution.

Chapter III

European integration discourse and identity

1. Central European views on European Integration

The discourse about European integration has been strongly dependent on the political and geographical context. The case of the pre-accession language and behaviour of Central European post-communist countries is an especially good illustration of this dependence starting with the very classification of the countries in this region. Until the beginning of the 'nineties there was only one concept referring to the post-communist European countries: Eastern Europe. Then, after a few years of political and economic transformation in the countries of this region some of them were mentally moved West, and both in the discourse of politicians and in the language of the media a new word appeared to name them: Central Europe. There is no doubt that this linguistic change reflects a shift in public attitude towards the region and a certain degree of awareness that it is lacking homogeneity. The countries previously perceived as Eastern Europe have been divided into Eastern and Central Europe. Basically Eastern Europe comprises the former Soviet republics, and Central Europe – the rest of the former Soviet bloc. But this was not the end of this discourse transformation. Soon, the category of "East Central Europe" appeared and most often it referred to all post-communist countries aspiring to membership of the European Union. In this way the Baltic states – Estonia, Latvia, and Lithuania – have been linguistically incorporated into one broader political and geographical entity. Moreover, this linguistic operation sometimes supposed that the object called East Central Europe is just the Eastern part of Central Europe which, due to a kind of symbolic imperative, cannot be excluded from the European Union. Of course, all these linguistic distinctions presented so far refer to the ideal shape of the whole discourse. In fact many authors still talk about Eastern Europe as opposed to Western Europe in the sense established during the cold war era. Some others, referring to the same region, choose to write about "East Central Europe". To make everything even more confusing Central Europe started to mean more than the former non-Soviet countries in the "Eastern bloc". After all both Germany and Austria identified themselves as Central European countries well before cold war divisions intruded into the history of the continent, and at the beginning of the XXth century the concept of *Mitteleuropa* was far more than just the German geographical name of this part of the continent.

In this way matters of discourse started to touch further important issues, and among them the identity of countries in the region (on both sides of the present borders of the EU), along with identification of their cultural links and political interests. With the boundaries of Central Europe resuming their earlier meaning and including Austria and Germany, the whole Central European region received new status and, possibly, new significance in the present and future structure of the European Union.

There is no doubt that the perception of East Central Europe differs depending on the location of the observer. For the inhabitants of Western Europe the other part of the continent seems to be a troublesome remnant of a difficult past. It is surprising how close this perception is to the historical category of "barbarians", at least in terms of fears and general stereotypes. Those fears and stereotypes are firmly rooted in the brutal facts: economic development that is lagging behind, and significantly lower standards of living. At the same time some of the recent works of historians point out that East Central Europe cannot be detached from the rest of Europe if we are to get the correct picture of the continent. According to those authors neither the history of Europe nor its culture can be properly understood without its Eastern heritage (Davies, Norman, 1996; 1-46). Such a view is certainly shared by most of the inhabitants of the disputed region. To make the whole issue still more complicated some other authors suggest that the part of the continent which we call here East Central Europe has been divided by radical civilizational differences and happens to be the area of one of the possible clashes of civilisations (Huntington, Samuel P., 1996). Events in the area at the end of the XXth century, that is the war in the Balkans, seem to support this idea; religious differences did prove to be a significant factor in conflicts in former Yugoslavia as predicted by Huntington (although it is not enough to make us accept the clash of civilization hypothesis).

The prospect of entering the EU happened to be one of the very few elements that united the countries of East Central Europe despite the obvious differences and substantial number of misunderstandings between them with regard to perception of the whole process of European integration. Let us look at the pre-accession attitudes of the Polish public towards the prospect of Poland's integration with the EU. Such an analysis can serve as a kind of case study although Poland has of course its own peculiarities.

The issue of Poland's participation in the process of European integration appeared in public discussions in Poland well before such participation could have any basis in existing political reality. Already in the 'eighties a number of statements and press interviews given by representatives of the Polish opposition at that time it was an illegal opposition and by representatives of some Polish NGOs stressed the necessity of changing the political location of the Polish state within the European context [3]. Some of them openly pointed out that participation of Poland in the process of European integration was an absolute priority that could be compared only with the acceptance of Christianity by the early Polish state in the tenth century[4] . One should remember that in the 'eighties in the popular perception of the political situation practically nothing indicated that the division of the world into two antagonistic blocks represented by NATO and Warsaw Pact could soon be ended. What, then, were the reasons for such early, strong pro-European attitudes within the Polish elite?

These attitudes have their roots in Polish history, traditions and culture (Niżnik, Józef, 1991; 20-41, Niżnik, Józef and Skotnicka-Illasiewicz, Elżbieta (1992)). And all these factors were marked in post-war national education which never ceased to stress strong ties with Western Europe. In the present text national education does not necessarily mean only official programmes of education offered by schools. It certainly includes the influence of the family and the Catholic Church which managed to maintain its independence throughout the period of communist rule, adopting in fact the position of the only open opposition existing in the communist world. In addition, official programmes never eliminated crucial elements of Polish attachment to Western Europe. Even during communist rule, Poland managed to maintain educational exchanges with the Western world and preserve research centres cultivating studies in the social sciences and philosophy, studies which in most other communist countries were completely suppressed in favour of dialectical and historical materialism.

Strong identification with the European tradition was a significant part of the ideological background for the Solidarity movement which in 1980-1981 brought communist rule to the edge of collapse, and in 1989 successfully replaced it. But equally strong support for the European aspirations of Poles have been expressed by leaders of the left-oriented political parties, including those which offered shelter to many of the members of the former communist party. Therefore, the results of the public opinion polls, which showed the increasing support of Polish society for integration with the EU – reaching 80% in 1996 – should not come as a surprise. Quite another thing is the popular

---

3   In 1988 the Polish Association for the Club of Rome initiated cooperation with the German Association for the Club of Rome in research on the integration of Europe. One of the effects was a German-Polish seminar in February of 1989 and the subsequent special issue of World Futures, vol.29, No.3 (1990), entitled "The Future of European Integration", Guest Editors: Witold Czartoryski, Uwe Möller and Józef Niżnik.

4   Interview given by the present author to "Przegląd Tygodniowy" weekly, nr 20 (327), 1989

understanding of the possible effects of such integration. The political and economic elites seemed to understand fully that the accession of Poland to the EU depended on the political will of the members of the EU and would create variety of problems stemming from disparities in the level of economic development and civilizational advancement (Sadowski, Zdzisław L., 1993). But the common perception of the prospects for Poland's integration with the EU were dominated by a strong hope that this integration would lead to rapid improvement of the national economy and the standard of living. Although the results of sociological studies and debates in the media indicate that there was some awareness of the problems of the inadequate competitiveness of Polish industrial production and Polish agriculture, the majority of the society seemed to believe that the low costs of labour in Poland would secure economic success within a fully open European market. The first years of membership confirmed that those beliefs were quite right. Therefore, all the protectionist measures adopted by the EU before accession, that at the time were still in place despite signature by Poland of a treaty of association with the EU, were perceived as unjustified. There was a common belief that a certain asymmetry – in favour of Poland – in the levels of protection of the Polish and EU markets was a better solution than increase of European Union's subsidies. The fear of European Union protectionism had been present already in the very early discussions (Jankowiak, Janusz, 1989). In general there was a tacit expectation that in order to lower the costs of integration of Poland within the EU, concessions favourable for Poland regarding such fragile sectors of Polish economy as agriculture and the steel industry would be necessary. At the same time, however, there was a widespread assumption that the overall results, measured in terms of the balance of trade, would still favour EU countries which now enjoy a significant trade surplus.

Another factor present in the popular perception of the possible effects of Poland's integration within the EU was expectation that such integration would confirm Polish independence from Russia and would signal the end of Russia's hopes for regaining control over Poland in the future. Therefore, Poland's membership of NATO, which came before membership of the EU, could be one of the reasons that in 1999 the support of Polish society for accession to the EU dropped.

In general, in the popular understanding of the political effects of Poland's membership of the EU there was an expectation that it would increase the sovereignty of the Polish state. It seems clear that many of the supporters of Poland's accession to the EU did not realise that such accession involves significant changes in the traditional meaning of sovereignty. The language still used for thinking about and discussing the problems of European integration is far from adequate to the issue and belongs to the past. The observation, expressed well by Paul Kennedy, that the nation state is the "wrong sort of unit to handle the newer circumstances" is still quite accurate (Kennedy, Paul, 1994; 131). On the other hand, however, there was wide support for official efforts to build normal relations between Poland and Germany. There were no more room for the doctrine maintaining that strong ties with Russia are the only possible defence against the danger of German expansionism, although some fears of German dominance were still present. It seems that the effects are gone of the intensive propaganda which used this doctrine for almost half a century.

To complete the picture one should point out, however, the strong anxieties regarding the issue of free acquisition of industrial property and acquisition of land. These anxieties were clearly exploited in political disputes between some political parties, strengthening the attitudes which might have countered the efforts toward Poland's membership of the EU. Complaints against the process of "buying out" Polish factories (in the process of privatisation) and Polish land happened at the time to be convincing arguments in election campaigns. Experience showed, however, that as soon as the campaign ended these arguments disappeared from the political discourse. But still, in the summer of 1999 the official position of the Polish negotiating team for accession to the EU, pointed to the ownership of land as one of the issues which would be the object of demands for delays in adopting EU law.

The case of Poland shows that the whole process of integration of East Central Europe with the EU was full of ambiguities. The strong desire for integration went together with a low level of relevant knowledge, and some of the expectations of the public were clearly closer to wishful thinking than to realistic possibilities. Although most of the fears concerning the process of integration seemed to be unjustified, those fears were present in human minds and had some basis in the history of the region. Therefore they were certainly an important factor in creating further attitudes toward European integration. In addition, all the uncertainties concerning the future development of European integration were widely used in political games by newly formed political parties in the region. They were especially handy in the demagogic language of some of nationalistically oriented parties. The period of Meciar's rule in Slovakia offers an excellent example.

Apart from the demagogy of the nationalists we cannot deny that the process of European integration and the prospect of East Central European countries' accession to the EU created a completely new environment in which the issues of national and ethnic identities had to be thought over. At the first glance East Central Europe does not seem to be a special case in this respect. After all those issues became a matter of public debate in many of the European Union's member states such as Britain, Belgium or Italy. But there is no doubt that in some of the states of East Central Europe the European framework was decisive both for the process of rebuilding a nation's identity and for creating new relations with ethnic minorities. The cases of Slovakia and some of the Baltic countries are especially meaningful. Countries with a strong, established national identity, like Poland, the Czech Republic or Hungary also had to re-evaluate their history and their hierarchy of national values in order to fit their identity within the new European arrangements. Such changes have involved a difficult process of national education accompanied by a well elaborated adaptation strategy and a substantial amount of understanding on the part of European Union Member States.

East Central European countries' adaptation to the new architecture of Europe has certainly been strongly influenced by the requirements addressed to prospective members by the European Union. But the reaction of the candidate countries to the conditions of the EU greatly depended on the development of their political scene. After all, it was representatives of the governing elite who officially responded to those conditions. Also, newly created political parties were interested in developing public support for the idea of European integration and their countries' accession to the European Union. Therefore, eastward enlargement of the EU has at least in part depended on the speed at which the political systems in East Central Europe have arrived at maturity while a variety of factors affect the region through global communication. The main challenge was certainly the task of becoming "Europeans".

2. Identity and citizenship

Looking for a new ideal of citizenship. The case of post-communist societies.

The present section of the current chapter will concentrate on a very important dimension of identity: on identity created by citizenship. The new members of the European Union from its future Eastern peripheries add a new problem to the already complicated issues of both identity and citizenship. It seems that this is one of the areas where some elements of the communist legacy will reach the new Union.

The very concept of citizen seems to be an excellent example. Since its earliest meanings this concept has offered one of the most powerful bases for identity. Its significance was secured by its double dimension: individual and collective. Being a citizen has always been perceived as one of the most important characteristics of an individual but at the same time it has always indicated social and political location. At the time when the issue of national identity became a problem, the significance of citizenship appeared to be part of it. This has been especially evident in the countries where loyalty towards the state happened to be in conflict with loyalty towards one's own nation. The case of Poland may serve as an illustration. The following analysis will concentrate on the destruction of the ideal of citizenship due to the deformations of social relations under communist rule.

The dramatic changes we have witnessed in post-communist Europe have not only ruined some political and social theories and concepts (especially those of so-called sovietology). There are concepts – some of them hundreds of years old – that have been strongly upheld by these changes. This is especially evident as far as concepts of citizenship and civil society are concerned. These concepts have both theoretical power and strong relevance to social practice. They provide convincing evidence that the sense of political philosophy cannot be limited to the area of exercises of the mind. To be successful, all major changes in the social and political realm of the contemporary world must involve changes in attitudes toward the state and society. The attitudes that are most favourable for creation of a democratic system can be described by the concepts of citizenship and civil society.

Although the modern meaning of these concepts has a relatively short history going back to the European Enlightenment and the French Revolution (Baczko, Bronisław, 1997), we can trace some of their roots to the thought of ancient Greece. Aristotle's basic concept of "*koinonia politike*" used to be translated as "civil society". At the beginning of the history of European democracy, in the Athenian polis, the very nature of democracy was strongly linked to the ideal of citizenship. The basis of democracy was "citizen's wisdom" which meant the very specific qualifications of citizens, which are indispensable for maintaining the order of democratic society. Opposing the political ideas of Plato, Aristotle had to articulate this idea explicitly. Since then it has been present in different European political doctrines (Held, Klaus, 1993).

One of the most destructive effects of totalitarianism has been the destruction of the ideal of citizenship. In fact, we could probably reduce all the consequences of totalitarianism in the area of political culture to this one. In this framework, the whole dispute over the definition of totalitarianism is placed in a different perspective. For example, the question of whether in Poland, after 1956, we still had totalitarianism or "merely" an authoritarian political system loses its importance, since until 1989 the ideal of citizenship was absent from the political life of the country (Sadowski, Zdzisław, 1993). However, what really happened was not the rejection of the word "citizen". On the contrary, the word itself became one of the crucial elements of the new discourse, the "newspeak" of real socialism. But its meaning had been stripped of the most essential elements: elements of a specific knowledge, namely the qualifications that one needs in order to be a citizen of one's country. In this way the ideal of citizenship, which for centuries had created the basis for an open society, was replaced by the ideal of being a perfect member of a closed society. In communist societies being a citizen meant giving up one's personal freedom and being unconditionally loyal to the authoritarian state.

What are the qualifications that in the political organization called a state, transform a member of society, into a citizen? In response to such a question one could develop a sophisticated political philosophy. In fact we know of a number of studies of this kind (Riedel, Manfred, 1993). However, from a practical point of view observations that refer to the basic, if not trivial, facts, seem to be worth noting. Let me list three such observations.

1. In order to be a citizen one needs political knowledge; familiarity with the basic mechanisms that make a state work. Moreover this kind of knowledge must be a part of everyday thinking. In the communist state the overwhelming dogma was: "the communist party is always right". Sceptics could preserve some distance from such a stand, but still their stance hardly constituted genuine political knowledge. Generally, this kind of knowledge was obscured and replaced with rules of mythical thinking imposed on society, together with an ideological outlook, in a process of socialization involving a variety of means, including brainwashing (Niżnik, Józef, 1985;104-130).

2. For conscious citizenship it is important to be aware of common goals, the goals appreciated by the majority of citizens, while – at the same time – coming to terms with the belief that the individual constitutes the basic value. In this way the idea of human rights and the concept of the "*Raison d'É-tat*" can go together, since the ideal of citizenship has been aimed at preserving both the individuality and the common well-being included in the idea of the state. In communist states the supreme value is the collectivity of social life identified with the state. The "individual is rubbish", said Majakowski. However, the ideology of collectivism brought about quite unexpected outcomes. Attitudes arose which, in everyday life, tended to neglect the presence of others. In some cases collectivism resulted in an "insane individualism". Such individualism does not attribute much value to the individual person but stresses individual survival. This kind of individualism atomizes society, degenerates social relations, making them vulnerable to the totalitarian state. The power of the Solidarity movement in Poland at its birth in 1980 – among many other sources – was based on the discovery of others.

3. On the basis of political knowledge and accepted common values, it is possible that citizens can have the will to give up freely some of their personal, individual interests for the sake of the common good. This is a social contract forming the basis for a parliamentary democracy. In a communist state military and paramilitary forces, such as the police and army, secure the power of the state creating conditions for frustration, the alternative being giving up personal will completely.

While in democratic societies citizens' qualifications result in behaviour that is functional for the state and useful both for society as a whole and for most individuals, in a totalitarian state such qualifications are not valued, but instead loyalty to the party or compliance to ideology are expected. Social behaviour, in most cases, is a result of force or conformity, leaving room only for the "insane individualism" I mentioned earlier. Escape from socialism does not mean that society agrees spontaneously on new rules of social, economic and political life, including such important principles as competitiveness, efficiency and obedience to the decisions of a majority in parliament. Unfavourable attitudes toward new rules of social, economic and political order create social barriers to the process of transformation that may be more difficult to deal with than objective material conditions, e.g. the condition of the national economy or arrested civilizational development. I would like to argue that the social barriers to transformation that we observe in post-communist societies in Europe are the consequence of the destruction of the original ideal of citizenship including the basic qualifications which members of society should have in order to develop a civil society. Of course, the problems of social barriers to transformation can be articulated in terms of different theories: those of sociology, political science or social psychology (theories of attitudes are one possibility). But the primary conceptual structure that brings convincing insight into the social aspects of transformation from totalitarianism to democracy can be found in the ideal of citizenship; the concept that belongs to political philosophy.

Totalitarianism, by its very nature, imposes a specific framework for various aspects of public life and the functions of the state. It certainly determines social life, the economic system and the political structure of the state. It offers greater equality, but at the expense of freedom. It does guarantee some kind of order, including patterns for social behaviour. Also, it places people in a certain symbolic universe in which universe-maintenance is taken care of by specialized personnel (Berger, Peter and Luckmann, Thomas, 1966). Liberal democracy does this too although the mechanisms activated here are quite different. Unlike in a totalitarian society, in a democratic society the mechanisms of the state, in order to function, require quite specific competences both on the part of society and on the part of the political elite. In Poland, after several years of experience, we know that the conditions of transformation from totalitarianism toward democracy are by no means limited to the choice of political system. Let me discuss briefly what happened in the revolutionary situation that was created by such a choice in Central European post-communist countries. One can describe this situation as a "syndrome of withdrawal".

It is – first of all – withdrawal of the rules of totalitarian organization of political and social life in a country where citizens' qualifications are absent. At the same time it is the withdrawal of persons from posts in administration when there are no qualified personnel able to replace them. And it is the withdrawal of the detailed supervision of individual life that people had learned to live with and – to certain extent – even to profit from. This last factor is especially important. People in communist countries were deprived of the scope to develop initiative. In fact they learned not to have any initiative.

But, totalitarianism not only made it impossible for "citizens' qualifications" to appear. In societies strong enough to oppose it, as in the case of Poland, it resulted in the development of anti-state attitudes and qualifications. In Poland, these anti-state qualifications were previously needed for more than a century to preserve national identity under the strong pressure of foreign powers during the time of partition of the country. Patterns of social behaviour demonstrate a certain inertia. Time is needed before people will realize that the state now means something completely different; and that what was instrumental for undermining the power of the foreign, hostile state or for destroying communism or abolishing authoritarian rules, is dysfunctional in the new, democratic state. In other words, in post-communist societies which, in the process of transformation, entered on a path toward the democratic world, time is needed to develop citizens' qualifications. The lack of these qualifications seems to be responsible for most of the social barriers to transformation in post-communist countries.

From a theoretical point of view, such barriers are inevitable. After all, every social and political system tends to develop adaptive mechanisms that secure some kind of stability. When the system is radically altered, the very same mechanisms are turned into barriers that must be eliminated.

Transformation requires changes within the whole structure of the society and the state. Only some of these changes may occur as imminent effects of adoption of a system of parliamentary democracy. Most of them require systematic work directed toward changing the structure of values, human behaviour and human attitudes, as well as the whole political and economic culture of society. Institutional changes are necessary but not sufficient conditions. In order to work, parliamentary democracy, human rights, self-government, the market economy, and private property must be accompanied by the working concept of citizenship. In post-communist Europe this means changing "*homo sovieticus*" into a citizen. Only then will society successfully face all the developments that usually go hand in hand with political freedom and economic competitiveness, such as an increase of inequality or rising uncertainty in everyday life.

Introduction and development of the ideal of citizenship may appear to be a long process. In the meantime, spontaneous negative reactions to the measures that elsewhere – in developed civil societies – are routine practices of the state administration, can slow down the whole process of transformation. To a certain extent this is what we observe at present in countries of post-communist Central Europe. Attitudes toward privatization or new tax systems may serve as examples.

It was part of the strategy of Polish transformation, based on economic "shock therapy", to reach fast enough the threshold beyond which the positive changes in the economy, together with the new rules of political life would act effectively against social barriers and so make it possible to continue the transformation process. It looks as if this particular threshold was successfully reached. It is, however, still hard to see whether a suitable ideal of citizenship has had a chance to develop. In every case systematic educational work will be indispensable for years to come in all countries that are undergoing democratic transformation. This need for a massive educational effort creates new tasks for the social sciences and philosophy. What is needed is both a new symbolic universe and new universe-maintenance personnel. The subject of educational strategy embraces not only the new generation but most of the members of society. A society of educated citizens will be able to face most of the misfortunes that any country entering the free, but egoistic world may encounter.

The European dilemma of citizenship and the problem of identity

The process of European integration adds new problems to the issue of citizenship and brings back the question of identity (Soysal· Yasemin Nuhoglu, 1996). Habermas observes that it was in the XIXth century that essential change in the relationship between citizenship and national identity occurred; national identity became an ascribed feature while state citizenship was understood as the effect of construction of democracy. (Habermas, Jürgen, 1993;9). In fact, Habermas's observation has not proved completely accurate. The relation between national identity and citizenship claimed to be a new development in XIXth century Europe was typical for the XVIth-XVIIIth century multinational Polish state.

This is exactly why some historians suggest that this Polish model of institution-alized coexistence of nations in one political system could be useful for develop-ing future solutions in the European Union and certainly offers some kind of European tradition in this respect.

However, at the present time there is only one basis for citizenship in Eu-rope: the nation state. Even the European Union, when introducing the idea of EU citizenship, adopted the principle that citizenship of a Member State is a condition for citizenship of the Union. As it has been explained earlier, the prevailing ideal of citizenship has been strongly tied to the basic, collective identity of the people, that is to national identity. As it happens, in most cases this kind of identity, at least from the XIXth century, has been linked to the nation state. Opposing this view, one may argue that some kind of "soviet identity" has been developed in the former USSR but most authors agree that soviet identity lacked the most important features for identity based either on the concept of a nation or on the concept of a nation state. In the soviet state the dominating accent of collective identity was the supranational ideology, which led to the destruction of the traditional ideal of citizenship. The traditional ideal of citizenship is encountering difficulties also in the EU, although for different reasons.

The problems of identity and citizenship in the EU seem to form a very dif-ficult, if not dangerous triangle, which may turn out to be the Bermuda Triangle of European integration. This triangle is formed by the relations between citizenship, national identity and European identity. Since, for some time already, the ideal of citizenship has involved loyalty towards one's own nation state, the concept of *European citizenship* is lacking one of the building blocks of the moral dimension of citizenship unless the very essence of this ideal is changed. Of course, one may argue that loyalty towards the nation state does not need to be in conflict with loyalty towards the Union but – in this new context – the ideal of citizenship cannot be the same as before. There are more arguments to support such a view. Habermas suggests that development of a common political culture is most important if the moral aspect of citizenship is to be maintained: "Democratic citizenship does not necessarily need to be rooted in national identity of a nation; accepting variety of cultural forms of life it re-quires, though, sociality of all citizens within common political culture" (Ha-bermas, Jürgen,1993;17). In this view the idea of a common political culture as well as an ideal of citizenship is strongly linked to democracy. Since the governance of the EU can hardly be understood as a form of democracy the very possibility of European citizenship can be questioned. At the same time the new context for formal, administrative citizenship created by the legal European citizenship appeared to send an alarm signal for the fate of "active citizenship" in the European Union Member States. Martin Hollis describes the efforts made by the British Parliament to strengthen the active citizenship of the British by stressing its moral dimension. This moral dimension "would involve the ideal of public good and civic virtue which finds its expression in the largely voluntary contribution to society of citizens acting either as individuals or in association with one another" (Hollis, Martin, 1999;20).

As it happens, the classical ideal of citizenship is facing challenges from different sides. Destruction of this ideal has not been limited to the former communist countries. In Western Europe it has been replaced by the ideal of the consumer according to which individuals are related "through contracts made to mutual advantage" and which lacks the idea of the common good (Hollis, Martin, 1999;20, 32). Development of European identity may appear beneficial also for a new meaning of citizenship: citizenship exceeding the boundaries of the nation state and aimed at a new public good – the harmonious co-existence of many nations.

Chapter IV

Global communication and the identity of the Europeans

The title of this chapter is a little bit misleading. I do not intend to present European participation in global communication although such a task would be certainly worth the effort. Instead, I would like to consider the very concept of "the Europeans" as a problem. The phenomenon of global communication seems to be working towards solving this problem, and I am going to argue that global communication can be a crucial factor for the emergence of the Europeans as a category of human population bound by a specific identity.

It is clear that the problem I have to tackle is one of the relationship between communication and identity, and especially between global communication and collective identity. My focus will be on the possibility of further development of European identity in the context created by the global communication.

The issue of culture is one of the most important problems here. It seems, however, that the fear of a universalisation of culture, expressed by many world intellectuals, may be quite unfounded (Niżnik, Józef, 2007). The diagnosis of authors such as Ulf Hannerz that "there is now one world culture" is usually provoked by the world-wide presence of some cultural elements (Hannerz, Ulf, 1990;249). Globalization has indeed reached into the realm of culture but also in this area its impact seems to be somehow ambivalent. On the one hand, cultural diversity is still regarded to be one of the paramount values of the contemporary world. On the other, the signs of global uniformity of culture are more and more aggressive; from the omnipresence of blue jeans and coca cola, through the world-wide popularity of American films or pop music to world acclamation of the Nobel prize winners in literature or world recognition of the best known composers despite their cultural origin. These last examples may suggest that some kind of uniformity of culture is not limited to its mass form.

Numerous factors have made possible the universality of some areas of culture. Among them are: increased world-wide mobility of people; global media networks using the most advanced technologies (like satellite television or internet); and the power of the cultural patterns of the economically most successful societies. There is no doubt that some contemporary states are using modern global cultural infrastructure to their advantage, and their cultural production is becoming more and more popular and known globally. This is especially true of American culture with its film industry as the most notorious example. What is probably more important, though, is the way in which a single language, that is English, is acquiring a distinguished position in world communication. There are a number of reasons for this language dominance and not all of them are of purely cultural origin. But all those reasons are effectively amplifying each other: the attractiveness of the American way of life and American world leadership have created very favourable conditions for interest in American culture, while American dominance in science and technology has practically imposed on the world the leading position of English in academic communication and in the internet, which is as widely used for scientific information as for distribution of cultural production and promotion of Western values. Therefore we should not be surprised by inquiries into "cultural imperialism" (Tomlinson, John 1991), and the question about the possibility of a world culture acquires a quite different meaning (Wallerstein, Immanuel, 1991) .

We should not forget, however, that exactly the same conditions that made such questions possible have opened the way for the world presence of unique cultures cultivated in societies which until recently were almost completely unknown. As it has turned out, the global media and the cultural or scientific institutions of the culturally dominant nations appear to offer the only rescue for cultures which would certainly disappear without external help.

Although among the works of art that have won worldwide acceptance and acclaim there are examples of so called high culture, it is mostly popular culture that creates the image and landscape of the "world culture". But the global reach of modern media and the overwhelming world-wide presence of some icons of popular culture or some lifestyle details are insufficient to justify the use of the term, and pronouncement of a diagnosis of the presence of, a "global culture". Unless we limit the meaning of that notion to the superficial layers that – due to the global communication – are being added to the existing symbolic universes, "global culture" appears to be an overstatement.

Let me now say a few words about the concept of a "symbolic universe." The idea of "symbolic universe" has appeared in different contexts in the works of such authors as the philosopher Ernst Cassirer or sociologists like Peter Berger and Thomas Luckmann (Cassirer, Ernst, 1944, 1955, Berger, Peter and Thomas Luckmann, 166). What is common to all its applications is an assumption that a coherent worldview, represented by a set of meanings and values, is a fundamental need of human beings (Niżnik, Józef, 1985).

Symbolic universes are not immune to the symbolic items that penetrate all cultures despite their differences, but such items, although globally present, seem to leave the essentials of local symbolic systems intact for a long time. This is why, within the concept of a symbolic universe the "global ingredients" of a cultural environment can be reduced to accidental intrusions into the dominant, familiar world of locality. In the long run such intrusions can of course slowly transform the scope of "locality". But for a "local consciousness" this transformation seems to be unnoticeable. It will soon be clear that I want to use the concept of "locality" in a much broader sense than is usually accepted either in sociology or in everyday language. Such conceptual change has some earlier inspirations (Morley D. and Robins, K., 1995).

Symbolic universes, rooted in locality, form the basis for the primary social and cultural identity of a people. One may even dare to say that the intrusion of a variety of global icons into local symbolic systems in some cases leads to a greater awareness of local distinctiveness. This is so because every disturbance in the coherence of the world accepted as "our world" initiates a process of adaptation aiming to restore the coherence of our symbolic universe (Niżnik, Józef, 1985;40). But, in the era of globalization, such a process of adaptation inevitably acquires a global perspective which, subsequently, tends to change the dimension of what is perceived as local. Confronted by world-wide commonalities it seems easier – to accept "European" – instead of Italian, German or Polish as "local." A global perspective – made possible by global communication – seems to be the best way to discover the affinities between the different although well-linked cultures in the European family, leading to the enlargement of the area of one's "locality" and, therefore, of one's identity.

At this point we cannot escape the issue of nationalism and cosmopolitanism since the emerging idea of "Europeanism" appears to be a "middle of the road" position. Discussions around the concept of cosmopolitanism create the impression that the only alternative to this concept is localism or nationalism. Is there a place for Europeanism within this context?

The issue of identity seems to be the key to a possible solution. It is precisely its capability of supporting identity that makes a specific culture suitable for the construction of a symbolic universe. "Global culture", that is global layers of local symbolic universes, seems to be unable to support any kind of "global identity." Of course, the idea of a cosmopolitan seems to be a prime candidate for the case of global identity. But most of discussions of cosmopolitanism try to avoid the issue of identity since the idea of "global identity" is nearly absurd.

It is exactly at this point that most arguments get into trouble. John Tomlinson is one of the authors who have expressed awareness of the variety of traps in this discussion but has himself not managed to avoid one (Tomlison, John, 1999). Discussing the position of Anthony Smith regarding national identity, Tomlinson suggests that "there is, perhaps no reason, then, why one's repertoire of identities may not comfortably embrace also the global" (Tomlison, John, 1999; 102). Later, however – placing a lot of hopes on the development of a "cosmopolitan disposition" – he is forced to acknowledge that a global identity is unlikely to emerge. The solution offered is to develop a cosmopolitan disposition along with the attachment to "the local." "We could cease thinking in terms of antagonistic binary oppositions and try to think about the cosmopolitan disposition as something that does not have to exclude the perspective of the local," suggests Tomlinson (Tomlison, John, 1999; 189). Ulf Hannerz appears to be even more radical. Concluding his essay on "Cosmopolitans and Locals in World Culture" he argues that cosmopolitans depend on locals and – from the logical point of view – such a relationship seems to be inevitable. This way we return to locality.

While a cosmopolitan disposition – though I agree with Tomlinson that it has a very positive moral significance – cannot become the basis for a dominant collective identity, locality can. Even cosmopolitans have their own local background, and an identity grounded in some kind of locality. There is no doubt that, despite all global and regional impact, locality will mean for many an ethnic or regional framework or, most often, simply a national one. I have argued elsewhere that the process of European integration will even favour development of national specificity (Niżnik, Józef, 2000). Should we then expect that Europe will become the basis for a primary collective identity? (By "collective identity" I mean an identity experienced by individuals and common within a certain group.)

To elaborate this idea further let me start by making a distinction between the "European masses" and "the Europeans", that is Europeans aware of their "Europeanism". The concept of "the Europeans" refers to a hypothetical, future condition of the European population, representing numerous nations and ethnic groups who will all experience a feeling of unity that would make European identity the primary, dominating indicator of their social and cultural belonging. Until such a condition materialises people inhabiting Europe will be, first of all, nationals of different countries. The current results of Eurobarometer bring the necessary evidence. From the European point of view this means that those people can be understood as the "European masses." Therefore, the distinction between "the Europeans" and "European masses" is proposed here to indicate the presence or absence of a European identity *in a strong sense* – that is, identity as a denominator of a basic social and cultural entity which offers a human individual the foundations of her or his symbolic universe. *In a weak sense*, European identity, as one of many identities experienced by nearly every human being on this continent, has been quite common in European countries for a long time already. The Europeans, as opposed to the European masses, will experience European identity in the strong sense explained above.

The "masses" that appear in the concept of the "European masses" have no direct reference to the theory of elites. But it seems there is at least one link with that context upon which I am now going to elaborate. Global communication seems to be – at least partly – responsible for a new form of "global stratification." This was accurately discussed in the 2000 Amalfi seminar by Hans-Peter Müller. The effect of this stratification is a specific kind of elite: a "global elite." A "kind of" because, in this case, we can speak of elites – as Müller says – "only in a narrower and weaker sense". Müller points out that "elites seem to extend their reach and influence by forming arrangements of interdependence and networks of influence and decision making" (Müller, Hans Peter; 2000;64).

Global elites indeed represent what Samuel Huntington called the "Davos Culture": "They generally share beliefs in individualism, market economies, and political democracy, which are also common among people in Western civilization. Davos people control virtually all international institutions, many of the world's governments, and the bulk of the world's economic and military capabilities" (Huntington, Samuel P., 1996; 57). In fact, the idea of the "Davos Culture" has been earlier well described by Ulf Hannerz as a "transnational culture"(Hannerz, Ulf, 1990; 244). Zygmunt Bauman – identifying this process of the "construction of a new, self-maintaining hierarchy with a world-wide reach" – refers to the awkward concept of "glocalization," coined by Roland Robertson, indicating that globalisation is possible at the cost of local masses (Bauman, Zygmunt, 1997; 61).

But why make global communication responsible for this kind of global stratification? Because it seems that global communication acts to the advantage of those who can communicate globally. And this capability depends on access to information technology but, also, on the availability of a common discourse within which to operate. This discourse is a source of meaning, for both communication and human activity, which takes the form of social and political actions and institution building. Therefore, admitting the existence of global elites, we have to also admit the existence of a global discourse. Global elites are the participants of such a global discourse.

The idea of "Davos Culture" includes one more interesting observation: global communication contributes to identity building processes. It is within the global discourse, in the process of global communication, that specific people are becoming aware of their power and influence as well as of their identity. Thus European participants in the "Davos Culture" – with all their cosmopolitanism – become *the Europeans.*

But what about "the masses"? Samuel Huntington estimates that "Davos Culture" is shared only by one tenth of 1 percent of the world's population (Huntington, Samuel P., 1996; 57). On the other hand, there are no "global masses": masses remain local. Therefore, representatives of global elites seem to be completely detached from the masses and, in many cases, can offer neither leadership, nor guidance even in their home countries. Here I apply the concepts of "leadership" and "guidance" as defined by Hans Peter Müller (Hans Peter Müller, 2000; 54) .

If it is true that masses are rooted locally, then what does "local" mean within the European Union or even within all of Europe? The meaning of "locality" certainly differs in different communities throughout Europe. But I want to suggest that global communication may initiate a process by which the meaning of "locality" is expanded from narrowly understood, ethnic or neighbourhood boundaries to the whole of Europe. There is no escape from "localism" as far as identity is concerned. However, the dimension of "the local" is changing due to the broadened perspective. Therefore, global communication can turn Europe into a local framework, able to accommodate most other traditional localities including regions or nation states. As the world gets smaller due to global communication, so does Europe – to the point where it will become "the local" for most of its inhabitants.

At this point some objections are quite justifiable. What will happen to traditional "localities", villages or small towns, with their face to face contacts, that used to be the main indicators of locality? It seems that with the breaking of the boundaries of locality due to global communication and its new media its role will be significantly changed. It is hard to say, though, what will be the nature of this change. However, what seems already sure is that distance and proximity will lose their present meaning in a process called by Tomlinson and other sociologists deterritorialization (John Tomlison, 1999;106, Giddens, Anthony, 1991).

The success of European integration will largely depend on turning the European masses into "the Europeans". In other words, true integration means further development of European identity. What I have in mind is an identity strong enough to create an irreversible feeling of social and cultural unity among people living together within the European Union or perhaps within Europe in general. European identity does not eliminate other forms of self-perception since, as we know, everyone experiences a number of different identities. Sociological analysis demonstrates, however, that there is usually one dominating identity with unique characteristics: it organises our symbolic universe, creating the main " points of reference" needed by every member of society.

In present day Europe we still witness a kind of rivalry between different identities that attempt to perform precisely this role. Candidates for the status of the primary force organising the symbolic universe of the people living in Europe are – depending on the geographic, cultural or political context –

regional identity, national identity, and European identity. Most authors discussing the relations between these identities agree that they not only coexist but, in fact, reinforce one another. Anthony D. Smith, concluding his well-known book on national identity, suggests that "a cultural pan-nationalist movement to create large-scale continental identities may actually reinvigorate the specific nationalisms of ethnies and nations within the demarcated culture area" (Smith, Anthony D.,1991; 176). I myself have stressed the possibility that the diversity of ethnic identities in Europe "may become an important factor in the development of the need for one, common identity" (Niżnik, Jozef, 2000;395) . Within the conceptual framework of this chapter, one would be justified in acknowledging the existence of *the Europeans* only if the dominant factor organising their symbolic universe was European identity.

The process of development of European identity has been ongoing ever since Europe appeared as an idea and value (Delanty, Gerard 1995). At present there are two major factors that may significantly affect this process. One is the revival of national and ethnic identities and the other is global communication. As it happens, both these factors now influence the process of identity building somewhat jointly. Global communication appears to expand our symbolic world while the revival of national identity manifests its limits and shortcomings as an organizing force in the emerging new symbolic universes. In the case of Europe, only European members of the global elite are now able to operate comfortably in this new world while the gap between the elite and the masses in Europe seems to widen. Global communication may change this tendency, bringing to the European masses an awareness of the situation and helping in the development of an identity capable of coping with the global context. One of the important barriers may turn out to be the conceptual apparatus.

Communication may have achieved global reach in the technological sense, but this does not mean that it possesses the conceptual tools which would appropriately and sufficiently permit mutual understanding on a global scale, for it turns out that human beings are not keeping pace with the technological changes they themselves have been creating. In a sense, we are reaching the limits of our efficiency in communication, especially in the realm of discourse we have at our disposal. The danger created by such a situation should not be underestimated. Communication specialists are probably right when they say that "disorder in society originates in disorder in communication" (Dunkan, H.D.,1968;130).

Yet, the language – that most important tool of communication, and, therefore, of social coexistence – which we use to describe our contemporary international reality, has been shaped in a world that already belongs to the past. Its main points organizing our discourse are concepts of nation state, borders, sovereignty, military domination, etc. Before our very eyes, these notions are either losing their applicability or changing their meaning to such a degree that using them leads to misunderstandings which, in the social sphere, means conflicts and destabilisation.

Our linguistic habits are such that at a time when large-scale military confrontation is becoming less and less probable, we use the discourse of war to describe economic competition. Paul Kennedy notes that "the language used to describe international trade and investment today has become increasingly military in nature; industries are described as coming 'under siege,' markets are 'captured' or 'surrendered.'" (Kennedy, Paul, 1993; 127) And sometimes this language is a manifestation of unparalleled hypocrisy. Countries which remain far behind the world of the rich and well-to-do are called "developing countries." This term is used in reference also to areas recurrently suffering from demographic explosion, famine, wars, and diseases.

Another source of serious misunderstanding in social communication is nondiscursive communication. For example, mass media – just by using images – present a one-sided view of the world, creating aspirations which subsequently collide mercilessly with a local reality, thus increasing people's frustration.

The area of culture and education – despite the information revolution – remains, to a large degree, a matter of local customs and institutions. It is exactly in this realm – that is, in educational and cultural life – that the need for ethnic specificity is being maintained and developed. Here global communication collides head on with local concepts of knowledge and local standards of education, as well as with local culture and local cultural policy.

Significant civilizational diversity is well-demonstrated by differences in educational and cultural needs and practices. Is global communication capable of eliminating the threat of the "clash of civilizations" about which Samuel Huntington has written? According to Huntington, "in the multicivilizational world, a constructive course is to renounce universalism, accept diversity and seek commonalties" (Samuel P. Huntington, 1996;318). But is it possible, in those countries where religious fundamentalism is being reborn, to create a cultural policy and an educational strategy that would guarantee the implementation of these recommendations?

All these problems – from the inadequate political discourse to the need for appropriate educational and cultural policy – are still left to national governments, and contribute to the stratification effect in global communication. As a consequence, traditional boundaries of localities are maintained, limiting the scope of European people for participation in the global exchange of ideas and leaving them in the position of the European masses both in terms of their

identity and of their access to power. It seems that the magnificent communica
tion technology of our time is almost powerless when facing these facts.

This situation calls for action on the part of the European Union. I have in
mind a well-designed educational strategy and a well-designed cultural policy.
Currently, under the present legal conditions of the EU, key decisions in both
education and culture have been left to national governments. But this does not
preclude action on the part of the EU. With regard to education, the idea of a
European dimension in education appears to be just a postulate although the
successful development of the Bologna process may turn it into reality. With
regard to culture, very little has been done. Article 151 of the Maastricht Treaty
as well as the EU Culture 2000 Programme sound very declarative. The Lisbon
Treaty has not been a breakthrough in this area either. What is needed, first of
all, is a cultural policy that would increase access to culture for every citizen of
the EU, and an educational strategy placing cultural activity high within the
hierarchy of values. Then the expansion of our "locality" and development of
European identity in a strong sense would have a chance to come as a natural
consequence, because it would be clear how small Europe is and how close our
different national, regional, and ethnic cultures are. This is why global communication seems to be as much a challenge for European integration as an opportunity to turn the European masses into *the Europeans*.

Chapter V

Nationalism in European integration discourse

European integration has already been perceived as a success despite all the setbacks we have experienced during the sixty years of history of the European communities, and despite the monetary and financial crisis which hit EU in the second decade of this century. In fact one could argue that the process which ended with the foundation of the European Union is one of the very few examples of implementation of a project which at its beginnings could be correctly called a utopian idea.

But developing a utopian idea further can appear more difficult than its successful practical initiation. It is quite clear that between the construction of the vision of a united Europe and creation of a working society of "Europeans" there are a number of issues which cannot be solved simply by political decisions. European integration implies radical changes in the basics of the symbolic universes that all the ethnic groups involved have been building and maintaining for centuries. Therefore the future of European integration does not only depend on solutions in the areas of politics and economics. In fact one may say that the final outcome of the whole process will be decided in the sphere of human minds and in the realm of the symbols which are responsible for an autonomous and powerful world; the socially constructed symbolic world of group existence and co-existence; the world of sameness and distinctiveness, closeness and detachment. The traditions of the groups, their shared values and identities are part of this world. What will be its boundaries, socially experienced and accepted by members of the different groups? These boundaries – in fact – determine which differences are tolerable or even desirable and which are not, and who is a member of the common entity that transcends traditional ethnic units.

On the way to European integration, the national identities of the people of Europe will inevitably have to come to terms with their European identity. Both identities have co-existed since the idea of Europe in its axiological sense, that is an idea of Europe as civilisation, appeared. But it is the project of European integration which tends to change the significance of both. In discussing this problem I am going to focus on one of its aspects, namely the issue of discourse.

As the process of European integration goes on, national sentiments within integrating Europe not only do not disappear but seem to be getting stronger. There is solid evidence to justify such a diagnosis. In many Member States ethnic groups that used to express national identity but stayed within federal or even unitary states started to demand autonomy if not independence. The Scots and Welsh in the UK or the Catalans in Spain are the most often cited cases but there are many more examples, and some of them threaten the very essence of the integrating process (Giordano, Benito and Roller, Elisa, 2002).

It is also clear that the response of the states facing such nationalistic demands would be completely different if not for the fact that both those states and their respective parts seeking greater autonomy or independence would remain part of the EU if such demands were successful. Of course, there are obvious arguments against multiplying the number of political units that are members of the Union but there are also arguments to defend such moves. Those demands are usually nationalistic at bottom but not without some economic or political rationale. In the present analysis however, the main focus will be not so much on "material", economic or political, aspects of nationalism but rather on its meaning and its role in the political thinking of both politicians and average members of society in an integrating Europe. Therefore, my attention will be concentrated rather on the problems of discourse, than on problems of political activity.

The term "nationalism" seems to be excluded from the European integration discourse, and if it appears it is only to indicate that something in the European project went wrong. Such absence may be surprising since this word has numerous meanings and some of them can be easily accommodated in the language used for description of important European issues or for theorizing on European integration. Contemporary debates about the final political form of the EU and especially attachment to intergovernmentalism with its stress on preserving the sovereignty of nation-states within the Union can be interpreted as the continuous presence of nationalism in the policies of many Member States. Of course, part of the reason for such attitudes are the well grounded values shared by the majority in their societies. Those values have been for centuries nourished by national education, traditions and mythologies and – in fact – in the case of many countries used to be instrumental for survival, both in the sense of preservation of specific group identity and also of biological existence. The example of Poles in this context is especially relevant, since their strong national identity and the high position of patriotism on the scale of values have been established at the time when the Polish state had been eliminated from the map of Europe and Polish ethnic territory was split among neighbouring powers.

Defence of sovereignty was for centuries a crucial aim among the basic goals of any state. However, as it has been shown in the earlier parts of this study, radical changes both in the region and in the world made it clear that the basic goals of the European states – including preservation of the ethnic identity and well being of their citizens – can be better secured by the process of integration than by insisting on traditionally understood political sovereignty. In practice, the concept of sovereignty has lost much of its initial meaning of a legal principle or a political mechanism and has become in public discourse primarily just an abstract, symbolic value. It has retained, however, its powerful impact on social consciousness and has therefore continued to be an effective instrument in social communication (Niznik 2006b:39) .

In the present considerations I have to distinguish among the different research tasks that may involve the issue of nationalism. First, is the analysis of the concept of nationalism, in its variety of linguistic applications. Next, comes identification and analysis of the "problem" of nationalism, which is a matter of certain attitudes, beliefs and stereotypes and refers to relations between different ethnic groups, different states or competing political orientations within the same state. Still different is the analysis focused on one, although probably the most important aspect of the problem of nationalism, that is nationalism as a sentiment. In fact, these distinctions are quite an arbitrary decision since they cannot be fully detached. After all, it is nationalistic sentiment which leads to social movements or to specific attitudes towards one's own ethnic group and to the "others" that in most cases create a "problem" of nationalism. Therefore those distinctions may only serve as a general indicator informing about the theoretical aims of the analytical work at hand.

It is clear that the problem of nationalism appears only when the concept functions as a primary social value and involves evaluations in social relations. Therefore, the problem of nationalism is closely linked to its ideological aspect, as explained later. However, when talking about "the problem" of nationalism I still have in mind theoretical reflection as distinguished from nationalism as a sentiment which refers to the social psychological phenomenon.

Legal provisions oriented toward "fighting" or containing nationalism very rarely use the word "nationalism" although the "problem" of nationalism is present in their background. Legal discourse sounds better when its literal aim is rather "defending" something than "fighting with". This is why those provisions usually deal with the human rights or the rights of ethnic minorities. On the other hand when "nationalism" is meant to indicate a social sentiment it usually describes such phenomena as xenophobia which in many cases is its direct effect.

This brief discussion shows how complicated the issue of nationalism is, and explains why theoretical reflection devoted to this subject leads to so many different ideas.

The problem of nationalism – perceived as a threat to European unity – is clearly present in the background of political decisions and ideas that were put forward exactly to counterbalance this threat in the integration process. One such decision is the institutionalization of European identity that started in December 1973 with the European Community intergovernmental conference in Copenhagen which has formulated the idea of European identity in order to face global turbulences of the early seventies (Bo Stråth, 2002). European identity meant there the location of Europe on the global scene, the hierarchy of its goals, and – what is most important – the scope of EC responsibilities in Europe and beyond. Such a use of this word has referred "identity" to Europe, not to Europeans. "European identity" was to be understood as identity of Europe, its specificity and general characteristics. Therefore, at the Copenhagen summit of the nine members of the EC the concept of "European identity" was used as a political term which had nothing to do with this very important personal experience, which is also called "European identity", and which is taken to indicate identification with, and the emotional attachment of Europeans to Europe. Of course, these two meanings of "European identity" can at certain points coincide. This is the case when "European identity" referring to Europe is identified with the idea of Europe as a value, which is certainly needed when talking about European identity as a personal experience that allows one to say "I am European". This distinction between European identity as identity of Europe and as identity of Europeans (that is identification with Europe) seems to be the basic one when talking about this issue (Delanty, 1995).

Sometimes, European identity in this second meaning used to be proposed as an alternative to national identity – supposedly – threatening individual attachment to one's ethnic group. Such a perspective, which presents the national and the European as contradictory, conceals the fact that everyone shares many identities, and moves the whole discourse into the area of "ideological" nationalism. In fact there are no arguments that would justify such opposition unless one adopts the discourse organized around the concept of a nation. In the present text I will try to show that most of the discussions about European integration that present the European process and national specificity as rival aims contradicting each other are based on a misunderstanding, although sometimes such understanding is quite consciously intended, since it may always count on striking a chord with very strong group sentiments associated with the idea of a nation. It should be stressed that rejecting the opposition of European and national identity does not mean that the idea of national identity and its emotional psychological social context should be also rejected. On the contrary, underestimation of the social role of national feeling may be a serious barrier to the proper understanding of any process of political integration including European integration. For example, for most of the Central-Eastern European post-communist countries European integration has been perceived as the ultimate escape from soviet and later Russian domination. Therefore, the aim to preserve national distinctiveness and the wish to co-decide about a country's future were among the most important motives for accession to the EU. Those clearly nationalistic reasons for joining the integrating Europe have still to be accommodated within the whole integration process including decisions regarding final political form of a united Europe. There is no doubt that this will need quite a dramatic change in the mentality of all Europeans since societies of "old Europe" also demonstrate nationalistic sentiments, although their nature is quite different from those of newly accepted members. I am going to discuss the problems of European and national identity in the next part of this chapter.

Apart from the discourse centred on the process of integration it is almost impossible to avoid common phrases that have grown up from understanding nationality as a cultural and social fact, such as "national character". The concept of national character appears mostly in everyday, common language and – depending on the context – may indicate quite different aspects of group characteristics. Most often it refers to national stereotypes (when used by outsiders) or to self-perception (when used by the members of the given ethnic group). "National character" very rarely appears in academic works. One of the exceptions is a brief comment by Karl Deutsch, who locates this term in the discussion over the role of culture as a denominator of the nation and understands it as a synonym of patterns of culture typical for the ethnic group (Deutsch, 1966: 37).

The present text is aimed at investigation of the very concept of nationalism. Therefore, nationalism as a problem or nationalism as a kind of social sentiment will be of interest to me only in so much as it will be the outcome of analysis of the concepts studied. It is clear that at least some authors use the word "nationalism" as a technical, descriptive, neutral term, which does not necessarily lead to a "problem of nationalism". In fact this is the case of the theories of three of the authors to be discussed later: Ernest Gellner, Karl Deutsch and Benedict Anderson. Although each of them can be useful in explaining or even handling the problem of nationalism, none of them present this phenomenon as an inevitable social illness.

Karl Deutsch's approach is especially interesting despite the time that has passed since his dissertation devoted to this topic was written. There are several reasons for that. **First**, Deutsch made an effort to make the phenomenon of nationalism measurable. Although the results were far from satisfactory his methodological attempts are quite unique among the studies of this issue. It is quite clear that his ambitions for measurability led him to the **next** interesting conception, that is the crucial role of social communication in emerging nationalism. Deutsch's idea was to use the concept of information as the basic unit in communication. In this way communication itself, its level of intensity and its content could be measured indicating the "intensity" of nationalism itself. The way to do this was to measure the flow of information, losses or distortions of units of information. After more than fifty years and with new methods of discourse analysis these hopes of Deutsch seem to be quite simplistic if not naïve. But in the middle of the XXth century the dominant requirement of American sociology was to make it fully empirical. The way to do this in the area studied by Deutsch was to concentrate on whatever was observable. "What we are interested in here – writes Deutsch – is the observable ability of certain groups of men and women to share with each other a wide range of whatever might be in their minds, and their observable inability to share these things nearly as widely with outsiders" (Deutsch 1966: 91). In this very quotation one may notice a **still further peculiarity** of his theory, and this is the unclear relation between two concepts: "nationalism" and "nationality", which are supposed to be explained by those "observable abilities". In fact, in many places Deutsch is using these concepts as synonyms. However, the primary concept seems to be "nationalism" and "nationality" appears as a form of social identity organized around the idea of nationalism. This is why Deutsch needed the concepts of society and culture, which also had been defined in a quite a specific way. "Societies produce, select and channel goods and services. Cultures produce, select, and channel information. A railroad or a printing press is a matter of society. A traffic code or an alphabet is a matter of culture", we read (Deutsch 1966: 92). It is easy to define culture in a quite different way and include railroads and the printing press as its elements. In fact this would be closer to the understanding of culture typical for cultural anthropologists. Of course, the author under discussion needed his distinction to proceed with his main idea, which was focused on the role of social communication.

A common culture, according to Deutsch, is what makes communication possible and, in effect, the people involved are turned into a community, that is a group of individuals who share the same nationality. The idea of social communication as the decisive factor in founding a feeling of national identity seems to be worth further elaboration especially in the new context created by European integration. Therefore I will return to it in the following section of the present text. Deutsch himself calls such understanding of nationality "a functional definition of nationality" since whenever we observe an effective social communication we can talk about a distinct "nationality". In this way a place for nationalism has been created. In fact such "functional" definition is what puts the phenomenon of nationalism before the phenomenon of nation. This problem has not been directly discussed by Deutsch but has become an important mark of the theory of Ernest Gellner, who claimed that "It is nationalism which engenders nation, and not the other way round" (Gellner, 1983:55). Let me then move now to some of the ideas of the author of "Nations and Nationalism".

Among the many definitions of nationalism probably the most useful one is that by Ernest Gellner: "Nationalism is primarily a political principle, which holds that the political and the national unit should be congruent" (Gellner, 1983:1). This definition happens to be a good basis for investigating other meanings of this concept. Gellner himself suggests that both nationalism as a sentiment and nationalism as a movement can be defined in reference to this principle. The reason for the usefulness of this principle is its neutrality which in the case of nationalism is not a common approach. Of course, as soon as we move from descriptive use of the concept toward the area of social sentiments its neutrality immediately disappears. Even within Gellner's intended neutrality some problems are unavoidable. The expected congruency is in fact difficult to achieve for many reasons, for example because of ethnic minorities within the state, or intensive migration. This is why in political reality nationalism has been most often identified as a problem and a possible cause of conflicts. An accusation of nationalism usually implies intolerance to other ethnic groups, and irrational attachment to one's own. Although social sciences have offered theories like that of Gellner, with clearly neutral, descriptive senses of the term, in everyday language "nationalism" usually indicates a phenomenon with almost inevitable negative social and political effects. Such understanding of nationalism refers to meanings which have a strong ideological character.

The ideological aspect of nationalism can be referred to a variety of elements of this phenomenon and to different senses of the concept of ideology. Among them I may especially point out a Marx-Mannheim concept of ideology as false consciousness driven by a wish to defend partisan interests (class interests in Marx theory) or ideology understood simply as theorizing on specific social ideas (e.g. "neoliberal ideology").

In fact, the classical Marx-Mannheim approach happened to be useful in some important writings. Ernest Gellner, for example, stressed that "nationalist ideology suffers from pervasive false consciousness. Its myths invert reality: it claims to defend folk culture while in fact it is forging a high culture; it helps to protect an old folk-society while in fact helping to build up an anonymous mass society" (Gellner, 1983: 124). Further on, the author lists a whole set of declared aims that in reality appear to be replaced by actions which contradict them.

In the present analysis I would like to offer a different understanding of ideology and recall my earlier redefinition of ideology, somehow going away from the traditional Marx-Mannheim concept in order to grasp another aspect of those social phenomena which are usually called ideologies. According to this redefinition the essence of ideology is an elevation of certain idea (in fact its concept) to the position of absolute (Niżnik, 2006c;77). In the case of ideological nationalism this is exactly the case: the concept of "nation" becomes the ultimate, absolute value beyond any chance of detached reflection or analysis. "In a nationalist age" – writes Gellner, recalling the views of Durkheim, who maintained that the worshiping of a society is mediated by religion – "societies worship themselves brazenly and openly, spurning the camouflage" (Gellner 1983: 56).

Ideological nationalism – whether in theoretical attempts or in popular sentiments – excludes the use of the term "nationalism" in an axiologically neutral, descriptive sense. Therefore it cannot serve as a technical term in social science's discourse. If it appears in academic work it has an evaluative meaning that is used to characterize quite specific, usually unacceptable attitudes and behaviours. This is the case of H.M. Chadwick's distinction between patriotism and nationalism, which has been cited by Karl Deutsch. According to Chadwick, patriotism means love of the home country and the desire to protect it while nationalism means "opposition or aversion to persons or things which are strange or unintelligible" (Deutsch 1967: 288 n.) It is clear that in such a sense nationalism implies not only a very specific understanding but also the emotional experience of a "nation" (one's own nation) as the only acceptable social environment for every-day life and in fact appears to be another word for xenophobia. The view of Ernest Gellner on the relation between patriotism and nationalism is quite different, since he qualifies nationalism as "a very distinctive species of patriotism, and one which becomes pervasive and dominant only under certain conditions, which in fact prevail in the modern world, and nowhere else" (Gellner, 1983: 138). In this way Gellner maintains his neutral non-evaluative understanding of nationalism, which of course does not exclude empirical cases of problems created by this phenomenon.

In drastic cases such nationalism becomes the basis of a doctrine and can result in dangerous policies that are aimed at extinction of other ethnic groups as in case of Nazism or recent nationalistic wars in many parts of the world, including Europe with its ethnic cleansing during the war in the Balkans in the 'nineties of the XXth century. In the present discussion I will deliberately leave aside such obvious, well known cases of ideological nationalism and will attempt to focus on those examples which demonstrate ideological nationalism but are trying to conceal its consequences for specific policies.

Some authors perceive nationalism as a form of action or, at least, readiness to act with specific aims in mind. In this sense nationalism is also a form of attitude. Already Karl Deutsch has stressed that the idea of a nation (nationality) implies "a measure of effective control over the behaviour of its members" (Deutsch, 1967: 104), therefore the crucial element of such a group's unity is effective social communication. The same observation has led Michael Hechter to a quite different approach, developing an "active" aspect of nationalism. He defines nationalism as "collective action designed to render the boundaries of the nation congruent with those of its governance unit" (Hechter 2002:7). Therefore, instead of the "political principle" of E. Gellner, cited earlier, which implied that nation and the state should be congruent, Hechter focuses on action. Moreover, although he refers to basically the same concepts as Gellner he prefers to talk about "the governance unit" (instead of a "state") and "the nation". Talking about the "governance unit" allows him to expand the idea of a nation beyond the realm of a typical nation-state, although he is aware that many of those units actually are states. His stress on action opens the way for further elucidation of all terms involved and leads to the following categorization of nationalism: state-building nationalism, peripheral nationalism, irredentist nationalism and unification nationalism (Hechter 2002:15-17). In fact, a sociologist by specialization, Hechter offers an understanding of nationalism in terms of political science. "Nationalism is, above all, political", he says (Hechter 2002: 6). Therefore, he explains most of the puzzles of nationalism by the political mechanisms of governance. According to Hechter governance may be direct or indirect. In history, in most empires, the only possible form of governance was indirect rule. The reason for that was the large size of the unit with very limited and difficult communication between distant parts of the polity and its centre. Indirect rule to a great extent allowed autonomy and self-governance in those remote units of the empires. When indirect rule was replaced by direct rule, the elites who were losing their local power in those distant areas were interested in developing actions insisting on self-determination: the beginning of nationalism. "Nationalism rests on the belief – or better yet, the ideal", says Hechter, "that individual members of the nation would be better off with self-determination than without it" (Hechter 2002: 30).

The problem with this approach is that in many cases such belief proved to be quite correct, since empirically many ethnic groups were indeed better off when deciding for themselves about their fate. Moreover, Hechter tends to use the word "nation" in a quite unclear way. For example, he refers to some illustrations from the Roman, Chinese or Ottoman empires to argue that indirect rule did not create a problem of nationalism, since efforts at cultural homogenization usually only follow the rise of direct rule. In fact such a belief appears to be quite common. Probably this is exactly the reason why so many politicians in the European Member States oppose the idea of a European federation (a European "superstate" as it is often called), and why the emergence of European identity is perceived as a threat to national identity. This issue will be discussed in the next part of the present text, so now I will move to some other ideas linked to the understanding of nationalism as a "collective action".

Anything that is supposed to be "collective" requires effective communication. This is why the ideas of Karl W. Deutsch are especially worthy of attention despite the fact that his book on nationalism and social communication is more than fifty years old and was initially written as a doctoral dissertation. Since its first publication in 1953 both concepts – that is "nationalism" and "social communication" – have become so much studied that the links between them have been to a great extent missed. New, influential works on nationalism by Ernest Gellner, Benedict Anderson, Anthony Smith and others have redirected the interest of readers toward new approaches. Also, over time some of the observations by Deutsch have appeared to be out of context due to the new developments in politics, as a result of globalization or regional integration, and some of his hypotheses have been verified, due to technical advancement, by development of new communication instruments like the internet. On the other hand, the phenomenon of nationalism suddenly became a problem in the completely new context created by the unprecedented advances of regional integration with European integration as the most developed pattern.

It is more and more clear that the new explosion of nationalism in the integrating Europe should not be treated as the same phenomenon as that developed in the XIXth century (Simonsen, Kirsten, 2004,). There is no doubt that nationalism within the integrating area of Europe and that elsewhere in the contemporary globalized world are quite different cases from those initiated some 200 years ago or even in the middle of the XXth century, when newly created postcolonial states initiated the processes that lead to "fictive ethnicities", which Balibar understood as "communities instituted by the nation-state" (Balibar, Etienne, 1996). In fact, in many instances, especially in Africa, those "nation-states" only imitated states established in Europe and reference to the "nation" appeared indeed to refer to quite a "fictive" social entity. Contemporary nationalism in Europe has a much broader cultural and historical basis. Also, national sentiments started to operate in quite different conditions .

Among the many reasons for this difference one may point out precisely two factors: European integration and globalization. Other elements of the process are the new powerful media and the new ways in which they are used by political elites. As it happens neither nationalism itself nor the political units affected by its outbreak are the same as in the past exactly because of these factors. In this new context social communication appears both as the most important reason for those differences and as the most important of their effects. In fact, most important contemporary ideas and socially relevant beliefs have been decisively affected by the modern media, which have achieved an almost unlimited range of influence and have proved to be quite resistant to outside control. This, of course, does not mean that the media are free from political involvement or political dependence. It simply means that they are more or less free from interference from political or ideological forces other than the ones that create their current policy. The overwhelming presence of the media has created a completely new environment for communication. Therefore, any disturbances or misbehaviour in this area must have a direct impact on the most important social values and beliefs. Also, it is difficult to imagine that politicians will not use these new opportunities to stir social sentiments that have good foundations in ethnic traditions, literature, folk stories and mythologies. Nationalism happens to be the most attractive option, and social communication the most important factor to be considered (Niznik, 2008).

The theoretical perspective created by Deutsch with its focus on social communication should, however, be seen in the light of his quite peculiar understanding of nationalism which is sometimes replaced by the concept of nationality. In this way both concepts have been intertwined but have received distinct meanings. There is, however, an important aspect of both to which I would now like to move, and that is the concept of national identity.

National identity

National identity can be discussed either as an individual experience or as an assumed phenomenon of a "collective" feeling. However, when the area of consideration is a discourse, the term is primarily linked to its second application since the category of discourse implies more than one individual. National identity understood this way inevitably leads toward the idea of nationalism which in the present text is my main subject. The task of integration involving different ethnic groups must directly face the challenge of this powerful feeling. According to Benedict Anderson nationality or nationalism understood as a collective sentiment may be perceived as "cultural artefacts of a particular kind" (Anderson 1986; 13). Anderson refers to his idea of nation as "an imagined political community" but the real question is what makes such a community, what are the conditions that activate the imagination in such a way. Therefore, his very appealing and famous phrase – "imagined community" –may be misleading. Its shortcomings have been shown by Anderson himself in the question ending the first chapter of his book: "What makes the shrunken imaginings of recent history (scarcely more than two centuries) generate such colossal sacrifices? I believe that the beginnings of an answer lie in the cultural roots of nationalism" (Anderson 1986; 16). The reader is thus directed toward the essence of the problem, the culture, while "imagination" is left in its true role – that is of a successful rhetorical figure. As it happened, the main factor that was needed for nationalism to emerge, was – in Anderson's argument – printing. "Print-language" was essential in building up (with the use of imagination) a unity among people that were unknown to each other (Anderson 1986;74-75). Another important factor was of a political kind. In order to create the conditions for emergence of national sentiments local or regional elites with different interests from those of the central power must appear. This was the case presented by Anderson of the Latin American states which emancipated themselves from the Spanish rule after local elites of Creoles realized that they would be better off if they ended their dependence on the European monarchy and so initiated actions that led to emergence of a new identity.

A quite different problem appears when we try to determine why existence of different nationalities usually goes together with nationalistic feelings which may be the source of conflicts, national stereotypes unfavourable to other ethnic groups or simply an abstract fear of others which is known as xenophobia.

Symbolic universes seem to function independently from the logic we are used to in our intellectual life. When the coherence of a symbolic universe is at stake all the phantoms that scare the advocates of peace, tolerance and co-operation among nations are usually put to work. Nationalism in its xenophobic form and the resort to stereotypes seem to be natural responses to the process of political or social transformation which requires alternation (in P. Berger's and Thomas Luckman's terms), that is a radical change of symbolic environment, a change which, in fact, means moving from the familiar world to another, completely new one. Therefore, European integration has to be perceived as a major challenge to the conception of our social world, and national identity is no doubt a significant part of this.

The idea of national identity has been often used by intellectuals and politicians as a tool for mobilising the masses for or against political or social projects. The effectiveness of such a use of this idea indicates that appeal to national identity addresses an important social need. Indeed, group identity is a basic human need and a major part of the mental structures that are essential for maintaining a symbolic universe. References to the idea of 'nation' seem to help that identity to gain a substantial emotional loading. Discussing national consciousness, Karl Deutsch, has stressed that it is a "political fact" (Deutsch, 1967:165). The political effectiveness of all actions that refer to national consciousness is probably the reason why methodological nationalism became so omnipresent in the social sciences. "Methodological nationalism" – according to Daniel Chernilo – "can be defined as the all-pervasive assumption that the nation-state is the natural and necessary form of society in modernity" (Chernilo,2006 :5/6). In the background of such assumption there is a belief that what makes organization of society into a nation-state necessary is national consciousness which serves as a basis of its unity.

Many authors – directly or indirectly – point out that the essential characteristic of national identity is its subjectivity. Deutsch puts it in a quite an abrupt way saying that the national consciousness is a matter of will, and he cites the views of Hans Kohn and Frederic Hertz; the first stating that "nationality is formed by the decision to form nationality", the other defining nation as "a community formed by the will to be a nation" (Deutsch, 1967:25). Michael Wieviorka, offering his "ethnicity triangle" as an explanatory scheme, presents national identity as a kind of tension between individualism and communalism which is mediated by subjectivism which makes the third pole of a triangle (Wieviorka, 1995:42).

From the subjectivist point of view national consciousness appears to be a phenomenon which is very sensitive to communication. After all, it has been developed in interaction between the individual and the group; interaction which is possible only due to a process of communication based on shared symbols. Deutsch, developing his arguments on the role of social communication, stressed the importance of both the unity of the symbolic world and its distinctness: "Cohesion and distinctness of a 'people' is a condition for national consciousness to emerge", we read (Deutsch, 1967:173) .

While many journalists and political scientists insist that the process of European integration must inevitably endanger the national identity of the nations of Europe, many facts that can be already observed may suggest quite the opposite effect. I have in mind a number of cases that indicate an increase of nationalism within the European Union's Member States. In some of these cases membership of the European Union appeared to favour development and institutionalisation of the national aspirations of ethnic groups within existing, established states. The recent developments in Great Britain with regard to the Scots or Welsh seem to be a good example here.

Although European integration does not seem to weaken national identities it would be unjustified to expect that the national identity of the people involved will stay intact throughout this process. If this expectation is true, the issue of national identity seems to be an excellent vehicle for the political arguments that usually accompany struggles for power. And this is exactly what we observe both in the European Union's Member States and in the countries aspiring to membership. The concept of national identity directs us immediately towards the meanings of other basic terms starting with the concept of "nation" .

The idea of a "nation" is one of the building stones of a specific discourse and is inter-linked with other important concepts such as nation-state, sovereignty, tradition, national heritage and others. It is quite clear that faced with the process of European integration this discourse is losing its adequacy. The European Union is made up of nation-states but a nation-state without guarded borders and without a national currency is certainly a different political entity than before. All the European Union's Member States are no doubt sovereign states; after all each of them is free to leave the Union at any time. But – on the other hand – we all have the feeling that "sovereignty" now means something else than before (Hedetoft, 1994). This is why the methodological nationalism discussed earlier is at present so much criticised from different points of view, and why Ulrich Beck proposes to replace it with "methodological cosmopolitanism" (Chernilo,2006: 11) .

Inadequacy of discourse used in the discussions of the issues of European integration is probably one of the main reasons for the confusions and misunderstandings that trouble public communication in this area. Sometimes this inadequacy is deliberately exploited in political campaigns. We certainly need a new discourse to address European issues in a better way. What then will happen to "nation" when other components of our traditional discourse, such as "nation-state" or "sovereignty" are clearly changing their meanings? What will be the future of national identity?

Our experience so far shows that the process of European integration is serving well the further development of national identity which, due to the changing European context, has been acquiring new, more refined meaning and new significance. New relations between France and Germany or between Germany and Poland which have been developed as part of the European project have had visible impact on the national identities of those countries. Although there are still enough examples of destructive nationalism in European countries, we have good grounds to hope that such examples will remain marginal and, in general, that the ethnic differences, which used to create conflicts and endanger the unity of the traditional state, will become assets contributing to the richness of the new community of Europeans. At the same time, however, the whole process (of European integration and changes of national identities) is often used by the political elite as a point of reference in political discussions and struggles for power. Sometimes deliberately and sometimes unconsciously some political leaders and journalists exploit the discrepancy between the present political process and outdated discourse to mobilise the public against further development of the process of integration. The threat to national identity is one of their core arguments.

Let me devote a few more words to the basic terms again. Political scientists are aware of problems with the definition of "nation" and all the terms that are derived from this concept such as "national identity". In the present discussion, though, I want to adopt only one of the possible approaches. Talking about national identity implics a specific understanding of "nation", the so called "subjective" meaning of the nation. According to this approach it is the presence of a specific experience of identity which determines the existence of a nation. One of the ways of understanding such experience is – for example – Benedict Anderson's idea of nation as "an imagined political community" discussed earlier in this text.

Another problem which has to be at least mentioned is the following. Should national identity be understood as an individual experience present in the minds of the members of the group called the nation or should we assume something like collective experience of identity? Although such questions of social ontology seem to be very exciting I will not discuss the issue on this occasion. I have to admit, however, that myself I tend to agree with those who perceive identity primarily as a matter of individual experience (Berger and Luckmann, 1966). Therefore speaking about "collective experience of identity" indicates only that a certain kind of individual experience can be common within a certain group. Of course we should not underestimate the phenomenon of shared experience. A kind of community of shared values and products of common culture overlain by a common language does create an important "collective dimension" to such a private matter as identity, but it does not justify the assumption of a "collective mind" or "national spirit". Of course this does not mean that we cannot use such metaphorical language. In fact it may prove very useful as long as we are aware of its stylistic role.

There is also a related problem which cannot be omitted here. That is the role of elites in developing and maintaining national identity. One concrete case has been mentioned above in reference to the book of Benedict Anderson. Within this perspective national identity can be understood as a kind of social construction. In most cases such construction is the effect of the activities of some of the members of the social group in question: nobles, revolutionaries or intellectuals. Of course socially experienced identity (that is, identity common within certain social group) usually has the strong support of tradition, customs and cultural heritage which sometimes effectively conceal its origin, presenting this experience as an "objective" social fact.

Studying the historical process of development of national identity we learn that for a long time the experience of national identity was shared only by some of the members of the social group which we tend to call 'nation'. The modern sense of nation seems to have been born together with the modern idea of citizen. For this reason some authors place its origin at the time of the Great French Revolution, which abolished radical social divisions and, introducing equal status for all citizens, created the basis for a new sense of the idea of a nation (Pomian, 1990). The role of intellectuals was already obvious there.

Since that time this role has become even more important. The new national identities which developed through the twentieth century in Central European countries like Slovakia or Ukraine, and in many postcolonial states in different parts of the globe, would not be possible without the creative work of intellectuals interpreting history or developing national mythologies and national ideologies. In Malaysia there is even a Ministry of National Unity.

Maintenance of the symbolic infrastructure of national identity is still in the hands of specific social groups. In recent times, however, traditional groups such as intellectuals or politicians have gained exceptional support from the media. This is why it is so easy to use this infrastructure now that the radical changes brought about by European integration have opened the way for new arguments in political discussions. In many cases the power of these arguments is derived from the tension between the new reality and the inadequate discourse which is supposed to grasp it.

Let us look at the interesting example of German intellectuals reacting to the prospect of European Monetary Union. A publication discussing the problems of European integration appeared in Germany some years ago under the title "Für eine Berliner Republik". The authors, Urlich Schachta and Heimo Schwilk used the issue of EMU as a starting point for a broad discussion of German interests involved in the process of European integration. Surprisingly enough the threat to Germany identified by Heimo Schwilk – the editor in chief of Berlin's "Welt am Sonntag" – was, above all, the threat to the sovereignty of, and even to the very existence of, the German state. "For whose advantage is the dramatic step towards giving up German sovereignty ?", asked the author. To stay on the safe side he used a variety of statements expressed by foreign commentators with special stress on the opinions of the French. "Maastricht is the Treaty of Versailles without the war", was for example cited from "Le Figaro" by this German author (Schwilk, 1997) . This reaction to the prospect of the disappearance of the German mark from the financial market is highly significant. The Germans were fully aware that the common currency is one of the most important unifying factors. Decisions about accepting such a currency within the EU and giving up their own certainly involved more than just economic considerations. Probably more important was the psychological effect. This is why after German unification introduction of one currency became the absolute priority and was carried out almost overnight. In the background of the text under discussion is an interesting assumption which can be verbalised as follows: national currency is extremely important for national identity. In fact, the hesitance of the British to join EMU may indicate a similar attitude. There is no doubt that national currencies for millennia were perceived as visible signs of sovereignty. On the other hand their present role tends to be overestimated. A

Polish president, the late Lech Kaczyński, many times pointed out the fact that the national currency is one of the fundamental indicators of national sovereignty, somehow forgetting that during the period of Soviet dominance Poland enjoyed its own currency but sovereignty was clearly absent. In the case of Schwilk's objections, the issue of a common European currency seems to be simply an introduction for more basic questions. These questions are: what will happen to national identity as a European identity develops ? What will be the ultimate result of placing the nation-state within the broader European entity? As we know, the answers to these questions depend on the final course of European integration which still remains an object of discussion. In order to articulate his fears Heimo Schwilk referred to another French comment, made by one of the advisers to the French government who suggested that "behind the European euphoria and desire for the Franco-German union there is a hidden will to bring Germany to annihilation and to solve in this way the German question once and for all" (Schwilk, *1997).* According to the German author the intention of the architects of European integration is to supply the Germans with a kind of "substitute identity", i.e. a European identity. Although developing such a European identity may indeed be one of the goals of integration there is no reason to assume that the final effect, deliberately planned, is to eliminate any particular national identity.

Certainly, some questions remain. Can European nation-states survive the successful integration of Europe in such a way that the state will remain the primary basis for national identities or should we rather look for a different reference, such as, for example, specificity of national culture? On the other hand we can expect that national cultures will increasingly contribute to the new identity of Europe. Therefore our earlier question can be repeated in a slightly reformulated form. What will be the significance of national identity as European identity further develops?

More and more often the issue of identity is becoming a problem both in discussions in the mass media and for the public, not to mention the politicians. Helmut Kohl, whom the author of "Für eine Berliner Republik" calls a traitor to the German nation, used to say that the policy of Germany with regard to European integration is not aimed at creating the Germans' Europe but a European Germany. This statement then became a slogan, widely used in discussions among journalists as well as among politicians. There were some sceptics for whom there was not so much difference between a European Germany and the Germans' Europe since in any case Germany will play a leading role in Europe. The overall result of German policy in the process of European integration, however, has so far been very positive both for Germany and for its neighbours. Daniel Burnstein, in 1991, characterised well the new

political situation in Europe after German unification, saying that "it appears
that Europe has won by allowing Germany to win" (Burnstein, 1991:52). It
seems however that some years later there were Germans who were not satisfied
with these gains by Germany. On the contrary, authors like Heimo Schwilk
perceived the whole process of European integration directed from Brussels as a
hazard to Germany. At the same time Schwilk advocated "fast integration of
young, Eastern European democracies". This is – he said – the "primary and
morally most important responsibility of the European Union". Obviously, the
prospect of integration of the Central European post-communist countries with
the European Union did not create any troublesome effects for the national
identity of the core countries of the EU. One is tempted to say that it may even
have appeared to be very positive in this respect. Is national identity, which is
supposed to be endangered by the developing European identity, the only object
of consideration of the German author, or does the whole discourse around the
problem of identity serve only as a substitute for quite a different issue? I am
going to take for granted the statements of the author and will go on with the
discussion of the problem of European identity.

   As it has been indicated earlier in this text the concept of European identity
carries an inherent ambiguity which in most discussions escapes the attention of
participants in the European discourse. It refers either to identity in its psychological sense defined in social psychology or – in a somewhat metaphorical
sense – to the idea of Europe. While in the first case we are talking about a
factor important for both the construction of the individual self and formation of
the social, collective entity, in the second case we are talking about the specificity of a unique product of the cultural and historical process, that is the idea of
Europe. In other words "European identity" may mean either an identity of
Europe or an identity of people. The problem is that these two, quite different,
meanings of the concept of European identity cannot be fully separated. The
identity of Europeans depends on the identity of Europe and moreover for both
of these, to exist means to be present in the minds of people. Probably this is
why – according to G. Delanty – "most discussions on the European idea fail to
distinguish between the idea of Europe and European identity as a form of
consciousness. The idea of Europe existed long before people actually began to
identify with it and to see themselves as Europeans" (Delanty, *1995*:4). Delanty
is fully aware of the problems surrounding the meaning of the concept of
European identity and although he also could not fully avoid confusions, his
approach brings theoretical implications which could possibly be turned into an
encouraging message. Here is such a message: Since the idea of Europe, as a
social construct, is a matter of invention we might as well by our concepts and
our activity influence the process of developing European identity. In effect

many of the values and symbols that are at present essential for national identity may become a part of a wider symbolic reference system that is an identity of Europe. Of course, such a successful development is by no means sure. Cultural differences contributing to the distinctiveness of national identities can appear dysfunctional for the process of integration unless appropriate educational policy is effectively introduced in the whole Union (Zetterholm, 1994). Such a practical requirement seems to be a separate issue exceeding the scope of my present considerations. I should, however, point out at least the concept of a "European dimension" in education which has been strongly promoted by the European Commission.

Let me now move to identity understood as a psychological phenomenon. What is the meaning of identity in this sense? How is it that we get one? Social psychology is quite clear about these questions. Identity is usually identified by the answer to the question "who am I". Development of identity is one of the main objectives of primary socialisation and is usually also supported by a secondary socialisation. Identities usually reflect social roles performed by an individual and therefore, in reality, within each self many identities coexist. The area of consideration becomes a little bit narrower when we move to ethnic or national identity. Children in Poland used to be taught a popular verse which starts with the words: Who are you? A little Pole. What is your symbol? The white eagle.

The power of ethnic identity stems from the fact that this identity belongs to the intimate realm of individual consciousness and at the same time locates a person, with the help of powerful symbolic means, within a social group responsible for its "objective reality" (in P.Berger and T. Luckmann's sense) . The symbolic universe appears to be the framework for a historic society as well as for an individual biography. Therefore ethnic identity inevitably has at least two dimensions: personal/individual and collective in the sense explained earlier (it is shared by the members of a whole ethnic group). In fact the experience of identity appears to be a phenomenon from the borderline between individual, personal reality and the realm of common, social reality. Both these realities depend on each other and this is why identity can be perceived as a process, and its dynamics reflect both personal and social history. This observation, with the addition of the inevitable factor of subjectivity, is the basis of M. Wieviorka's "triangle" mentioned earlier. When talking about European identity we tend to forget that the feeling of "being European" can in fact indicate very different stages of development of such identity.

National identity takes its specificity from opposition to group identity different from the national one. Hechter correctly states that "Nationalism ultimately rests on cultural distinctions, but the meaning of cultural distinctiveness is ambiguous" stressing the role of shifting contexts (Hechter, 2002; 96) . Hechter has in mind multicultural societies confronted with different policies of changing governments. Another contextual factor can be related to regional identity. In some cases a kind of tension can develop between regional and national identity. No matter whether we talk about "regional substructures" like Wales within Britain or Bavaria within Germany, both of which are parts of specific states, or about a "regional superstructure" like the European Union which consists of different states, "geographical – cultural – political" identity other than the national can create a certain psychological challenge which sometimes can lead to a crisis of identity.

This is why emerging European identity is the cause not only for some hope but also for some anxiety. As it happens, both – hopes and anxieties – might be based on mistaken assumptions. Let me then conclude this chapter with a few remarks about some of these assumptions regarding – again – the relation between European and national identity.

Heimo Schwilk cites the Swedish author, Göran Greider, who writes: the "Nation state needed centuries to develop in all its citizens one, national identity. The costs were high, in many cases the task has not been achieved..."(Schwilk, 1997). As the Schwilk's argument goes, the implementation of the Maastricht Treaty would mean wasting something that was the result of centuries-long effort on the part of nation states: national identities.

To summarise my earlier arguments let me say that there is no reason to believe that this is what we are facing. **First**, I would like to point out that in the process – in many cases a painful and dramatic process – which relatively recently resulted in the phenomenon of national identities, together with national identities the basis for European identity has been created. After all, European history has been a common history and European identity has been present for a long time already, despite all the conflicts and differences. Therefore, it seems that it would be more appropriate to talk rather about the changes in the European identity than about something that is in the process of emerging. **Second**, the new context created by Europe's integration is initiating the process of reconstruction of national identities. In fact contemporary changes in European identity may appear to be a stimulus for the revival of national identity in a new and different form. The recent outburst of national aspirations of the Scots or the people of Wales does not seem to threaten seriously the unity of Britain or Britain's participation in the European Union. On the contrary, it seems that British membership in the EU made these developments less important to the interests of the British state.

In general, ethnic peculiarities may contribute to the diversity of identities which may become an important factor in the development of the need for one, common European identity. Such identity at a certain point may become strong enough to legitimate also the idea of a supranational European citizenship, changing the meaning of citizenship which until recently has been reserved for national citizenship (Nuhoglu Soysal, 1996). Of course, I have in mind the idea of citizenship which would go beyond formal, legal meaning of this institution toward its axiological significance that has been so important in the ancient concept with its ideals of citizen's virtues commented earlier.

Let me then be an optimist with regard to the role of national identities in the process of European integration. In the present, global context, the process of revival of national identities in Europe may in the end become an important factor favourable to European integration. One may possibly apply in this context Hechter's term of "cultural division of labour" which, according to this author, "is decisive for the salience of national identity" (Hechter, 2002;96). It may appear that the concept of cultural division of labour is also useful for understanding this new development, that is coexistence of national and Europe-an identities, while both seem to be getting a new chance of advancement.

Chapter VI

European integration discourse and compliance with European norms: making a supranational order

The power of European integration discourse has been best demonstrated by the complex process of compliance with European norms. In fact, analysis of the relations between discourse and norms may serve as a theory of supranational order making. After all, the European Union is a supranational political system no matter whether it is perceived as a federation in the making or as a confederal system closer to an international organization. The debate between those in favour of intergovernmental governance and those stressing the need for further development of supranational common institutions and policies has been to a great extent focused on the question of how to build an effective decision making system while preserving specific priorities (different for the two parties in the debate) regarding distribution of competences between the Union and the Member States.

The discourse employed in this debate happens to be a medium which not only articulates specific norms but also imposes quite definite conditions to compliance with them. The norms agreed do not necessarily conform with one or another of those two attitudes regarding the form of a political system of the EU. Therefore, we observe a number of situations when the norms that are expected to be followed by all contradict – directly or indirectly –the political orientations (regarding the nature of the political system of the EU) of specific actors. Moreover, the meaning of fundamental concepts depends on the overall structure of sense of the specific discourse. As it has been shown in the earlier analysis, the crucial factor appears to be the concept that serves as an organizing element of the discourse. For example, "solidarity" belongs to the basic values of European integration and demands well defined norms that would make it a reality. No one within the European debate is ready to question this value. At the same time it is quite clear that depending on the specific political system of the EU favoured by the given actor, its meaning may differ substantially. Neverthe-less, there is a need for common norms that would lead to implementation of the principle of solidarity. Such norms are in place, for example, within different policies of the EU and also within tacit expectations regarding behaviour of the member states of the EU. However, at present, the concept of solidarity does not function as an organizing element of the European integration discourse. As it has been argued in chapter 1 such a role is played by the concept of democracy. In effect, the norms that are supposed to serve solidarity have been contested in different situations by different actors. The most interesting fact, though, is that despite such contestation in most cases contested norms have been observed . All stages of this process: imposition of norms, then their contestation, and finally compliance to contested norms had to find their place in the political discourse. Therefore, analysis of the discourse may be the way to explain how this is possible and what kind of lesson this case may offer for the institutional development of the EU as a supranational political system.

There are three points that I would like to discuss regarding this topic. **First,** I would like to point out that the whole issue may be discussed as a problem that appears when considering the role of political norms in the relations between domestic and international contexts. This kind of relation has become a theme for a number of studies (F.Kratochwil, 1989, Djelic and Sahlin-Anderson, 2006). **Second,** we should approach the problem of norms involved in relations between domestic and international contexts as one of the essential aspects of European integration. And **third,** the topic under discussion appears to be a very good basis for reflection on some of the methodological aspects of the disciplines involved. It looks as if the problems behind the topic under discussion may be quite different, depending on the theoretical interest of the researcher. Moreover, in the area of our present considerations there is an interesting transfer of concepts between sociology and political science.

Looking at the issue of compliance with norms as a case in the relations between the domestic and international contexts one has to notice that this relation receives its significance in the realm of discourse. Although norms imply specific behaviour, in international relations the meaning of behaviour is usually closely linked to linguistic interpretations or justifications. This is why in diplomacy political statements are so important. Within the adopted use of the term "discourse" the sense of any such interpretation or justification is determined by the discourse involved. Therefore, it is political discourse that empowers the language of politics, turning statements into political acts. Of course, norms themselves are rooted in a specific discourse which is only sometimes reflected in institutionalized normative systems such as law or custom. In recent studies it has been stressed that emerging "rule-making" in an international environment is more and more frequently based on soft rules such as standards or guidelines than on "hard" legal regulations (Djelic and Anderson,2006: 5). This is the case of making order through the international scrutiny of specific nation states in the practice of transnational governance (Dahl, 2007).

This kind of transnational governance has been well illustrated by the process of European integration which has opened a new field of studies. Through the whole system of incentives and normative pressure, justified in a specific discourse, international institutions like the OSCE, the Council of Europe or the European Union have enforced the desired normative order in a number of policy areas (J. G.Kelly, 2004, M. Dahl, 2007, M.L. Djelic, and K. Sahlin-Anderson, 2006). The role of a new discourse can be detected by examining some of the crucial terms. For example, as pointed out by Djelic and Sahlin-Andersson, what is sometimes called "de-regulation" is – in fact – "a profound transformation of regulatory patterns" (Djelic and Anderson, 2006: 6), indicating a completely new discourse.

This does not mean that institutionalization of norms in different, formalized forms, has disappeared. The European Union, with its variety of new legal instruments (e.g. "directives") may serve as a good example. This kind of institutionalization of norms happens to be a problem in itself opening the way to a conflict of norms, especially when we take into consideration the possibility of different normative systems and their relation in domestic and international contexts. In fact, the same norm may be expected to be observed in different contexts which are incompatible. The case of an international arrest warrant introduced by the EU and contested in many countries as unconstitutional may serve as an example. This example refers, however, to a legal, constitutional issue which can be solved by legal instruments including changes of the law or even the constitution of a Member State. We may imagine a conflict of norms that arises from a difference of customs in different countries involved in the same international setting. The custom cannot be changed the way we change the law and from the social point of view may even be a stronger factor in securing the social order or in contesting the norms that do not fit within the given tradition. Therefore, at least some of the social barriers to the further integration of Europe may be explained by incompatible cultural factors, which also make the political discourse in use inadequate to the new political reality. This problem, however, is very rarely taken into consideration by political scientists. One of the interesting relevant analyses has been offered by Dennis Chong who has analysed some ambiguities of rational choice theory created by cultural and social specificities that appear to be important but often underestimated factors of the decision making process (Chong, 2000).

This is exactly why compliance with norms in domestic and international relations may be treated as the essence of European integration in its social dimension. It appears that this issue covers many elements of social integration involving differences in national cultures, transnational collective aims and the process of developing a political discourse to offer an effective platform for social communication.

Theorizing on the process of European integration has brought political scientists into constant debate about the nature of this process. Since the process of integration is by no means purely economic or political, and demands interdisciplinary reflection, many of the ideas developed in this debate may serve as an interesting example of methodological change in the social sciences. Those changes are also reflected in the discourse that is being developed. An example I am going to use later will illustrate the impact of sociology on international relations theory and will refers to a new use of the term "socialization".

Norms may be understood as socially operationalized values. Although in different disciplines the definition of 'norm' may vary – in all its various applications– e.g. we may talk about moral norms, social norms, international norms, procedural norms etc., in the background one may find a specific (social, political, pragmatic, etc.) goal which can be directly referred to a certain value or certain set of values. In political science sociological analysis appears to be quite relevant and useful. For example, Merton's analysis of types of individual adaptation can be applied to the political behaviour of individuals and also to the behaviour of states in an international settings (Merton, 1982: 203). Therefore, studying the origin of norms in a specific social or political entity we cannot escape the question of the value structure of this entity.

Both in the framework of the relations of individuals in society and of the behaviour of political organizations or states in international relations, norms have their origin in some kind of a contract or imply such contract . Moreover, in both cases there exists some kind of coercion which is supported by the system of sanctions. It is clear, though, that the motives to comply with norms are not limited to the fear of sanctions. I will briefly comment on three kinds of motives: the power of tradition, the need for an order and the fear of sanctions. In fact, all those motives are interlinked. In society tradition, including custom, secures the feeling of order and its violation is usually painful because of the variety of sanctions every society has at its disposal. There are, however, norms which have no traditional backing but are still followed because they promise some kind of order. Such motives are especially evident in international relations. A good example may be the non-proliferation treaty. This last example is a good one for showing that for some states it is the fear of sanctions which force them to comply with the norm or at least to pretend such compliance. In the EU we have a number of cases when the fear of sanctions (or actual sanctions imposed by the European Court of Justice) force the Member States to comply with European norms. In addition, during the process of enlargement compliance with specific norms was the condition of accession. The so-called "conditionality" of EU membership became even a technical term in the European discourse.

In the social context it is the process of socialization which takes care of compliance with norms accepted in a specific society or a specific social group. Among the main instruments of this process I would like to mention education (in the broad sense, which includes primary socialization in a family), religion and law. The main goal of socialization is to maintain a specific social order. These basic, trivial comments are here necessary in order to point out the main aspects of an interesting transfer of this concept from sociology to international relations.

Representatives of constructivism in the theory of European integration, who apply the concept of socialization in international relations analysis, do not even try to justify or define it in the language of their discipline. Most likely this is because "socialization" has become also a part of ordinary language used in everyday life, which has always been treated as an open source of new terminology in the social sciences. As in many other cases, this concept has been taken for granted without much deliberation on its metaphorical meaning (Checkel, 1998). What is quite obvious, though, is its assumed function . Socialization in international relations is supposed – in analogy with the sociological application of this term – to guarantee an expected, desired order in a given international setting. The way to bring about this order is to make all actors involved – in this case Member States of the EU – comply with European norms. It is interesting that the same problems used to be more often expressed by a quite different discourse, which sometimes even merges with the first. That other discourse has been organized around the concept of Europeanization (e.g. Boerzel and Risse, 2000). It is clear, though, that although both discourses refer to the same problems referring to the issue of "conditionality" in relations of nation states (especially those aspiring to membership of the EU) and the European Union, their focus is on quite different aspects of European integration. In the language of logic we may say that they denote the same but with different connotations in mind. From this point of view "Europeanization" seems to stress achievement and civilizational advancement while "socialization" stresses a specific dependence and imposed rules.

It is quite trivial to say that international politics can be understood as a system of competing normative structures. A quite explicit case is demonstrated by American politics with its fight for freedom and democracy world-wide and by Chinese politics of cooperation based on "tolerance" of every existing system of power on the basis of the principle of non-interference. Of course, exceptions such as the treatment by the US of some non-democratic regimes which are essential to American interests in some parts of the world (like the Middle East, for example), clearly diminish the impact of the whole normative structure of American politics on the world scene. Nevertheless existing normative structures have created specific expectations regarding the behaviour of the states in international relations. From this point of view the European Union and the whole process of integration, including the cases of enlargement, are especially interesting.

For many aspiring countries as well as for most of the Member States membership of the European Union has become attractive enough for its normative structure to be adopted even when this structure collides with some of the norms of those states. Therefore we observe numerous cases of contested compliance, that is those cases when the norms have been followed despite criticism of them. Antje Wiener describes such cases as "Situations in which compliance conditions are challenged by the expected norm followers" (Wiener, 2004: 189). Contested compliance can be observed not only in relations of the Member or Candidate States with the EU but also in domestic politics when the interests of the ruling party happen to be threatened by norms that are in place due to membership of the European Union. One of the examples observed in Poland was the criticism, by the prime minister Jaroslaw Kaczynski, of some decisions of the Supreme Court. However, despite contestation there was no a sign that this decision could be overruled.

Antje Wiener has analysed two quite different cases which refer to explicit (Copenhagen criteria of EU membership) or implicit norms. Implicit norms are those that are assumed to be an obvious part of international relations. The example that was analysed was the behaviour of EU Member States and candidates when facing the American decision to start a war against Iraq.

Contested norms are not accepted but what does it mean exactly? It seems that there are three most important meanings of such situations. A) The most vague case is when the norms are simply not appreciated, not liked, for a variety of reasons: ideological, doctrinal or pragmatic although they are not necessarily incompatible with the normative structure we share. For example, such situations occur when a political party's calculations show that contestation of a specific norm can result in increase of public support. B) A different case is when given norms have not been perceived as our own. In such case the norms may be known but do not belong to the body of internalized principles. C) In the third case contested norms may collide with other norms that we share. Therefore, accepting such norms without contestation would lead to cognitive dissonance. Contestation is then needed in order to maintain coherence in our own normative structure.

These three kinds of general reasons for contestation of norms could be ordered in a more elaborate scheme to include more factors that characterize the outcome of the process of socialization. In fact, a variety of illustrations of this kind can be found in a number of sociological analyses. Let us see, then, what possibilities can be taken into consideration when internalization of norms, acceptance of them and following them are included in the analysis. In most cases good empirical illustrations can be provided by the process of assimilation of migrants or by social groups which violate the general norms of their society, such as some political dissidents, religious sects or gangs. Among the illustrations below there are also some that refer to "normal" members of society who, for different reasons, do not follow the general rules, like believers of the dominant religion who do not comply with the norms imposed by their religion, or tax payers avoiding paying taxes. The most problematic appear to be the cases of internalized norms which are not accepted. This is because sometimes we tend to equate internalization and acceptance. In the present discussion I would like to make a distinction between internalization and acceptance. Internalization is here understood as a state of mind which is the outcome of the process of socialization and may be out of the control of the individual. Acceptance is, in most situations, a conscious decision or a mental state of appreciation. Therefore, internalized norms that are not accepted indicate some kind of deviance or dissidence, and usually – in Durkheim's terminology – lead to anomie.

Acceptance and observance of norms of "general" society: possible outcomes of a process of socialization (examples).

	Accepted and followed	**Accepted but not followed**	**Not accepted but followed**	**Not accepted and not followed**
Not internalized	"Motivated" immigrants; the will to assimilate	Minorities under group control	"Motivated" immigrants; rejection of assimilation	Some ethnic minorities (e.g. Muslim traditionalists in the West)
Internalized	Fully socialized member of a society	-Believers (Polish Catholics) - Tax evasion cases	Some cases of "mental" dissidence (political, religious)	Deviance: treason, a gang's rules, some religious sects

The above table suggests that we should reflect also on the cases when internalized norms are not followed and even are not accepted, but in international relations the most puzzling is compliance with norms that are contested. In an international context the whole metaphor of socialization encounters some problems when it comes – for example – to the concept of internalization. It seems that internalization of norms depends on different factors in domestic politics, and certainly on political options favoured by different political groups, including political parties. Therefore, contested compliance includes all cases when norms are not accepted but followed. In the EU, such situations occur quite often. In any of the Member States different interest groups may demonstrate their dissatisfaction with certain norms and even get the support of their government but in the face of general rules accepted in the community such support may appear to be only lip service, and the norms would be followed.

Why are unaccepted norms followed? What are the reasons for compliance in the case of contested norms? The answer to these questions is quite simple, if not trivial, recalling standard sociological analysis and in a way justifying the use of the "socialization metaphor" in international relations. The debates in the candidate countries during their negotiations over the EU membership were full of very good illustrations. Those debates showed not only the reasons for compliance but also the reasons for contestation that was purely tactical with a specific electorate in mind. Among most important reasons there were the following: a) Compliance with contested norms which were the condition of membership or of participation in a specific programme (e.g. structural funds), was possible because it resulted in highly valued effects, political or financial, b) Violation of imposed norms would bring sanctions or losses, political, financial or moral, c) Compliance was possible, because contestation was motivated only by political calculations and had only a tactical function. Therefore, it was more important to contest specific norms than to disregard them.

According to Antje Wiener the possibility of contestation adds legitimacy to the social or political order (Wiener, 2004:218). This relatively simple observation brings an important insight to the understanding of international relations and the very nature of politics. It shows that some elements of political behaviour have extended functions that go beyond the substance of political debate. In fact the same aspect of political behaviour allows politicians to use some of their actions or their oral declarations for tactical aims. Debates about the nature of European integration or about specific treaties – like the failed Constitutional Treaty – offer many examples of using European matters for goals in internal politics. This was the case in Poland as well as in France and the Netherlands. As explained in an earlier chapter this kind of political behaviour has been possible because of the political reality addressed and the inadequacy of discourse.

What are the consequences of contested compliance for the normative structure of a contesting party, which, in case of European Union, most often is a Member or Candidate State, although it may also be another actor of international politics, e.g a transnational corporation? It seems that there are three main consequences possible.

a) Contested norms can be, after all, accepted. In such a case not only is contestation withdrawn but also a new discourse is adopted, and compliance appears to have a true socializing effect.

b) The opposite effect would be withdrawal of compliance. Then the norms are not followed any longer. This would be – for example – the case if Kaczynski's government had decided to reinstate capital punishment in the Polish penal code. In most cases, however, it is hard to imagine such a move since this would have very painful consequences. Moreover, one could speculate that declarations such as those of former prime minister Kaczynski are exactly an instance of contestation for tactical purposes, to satisfy an important part of the electorate.

c) One of the possibilities is also action toward changing contested norms, despite initial compliance. In other words we can imagine a case of "tactical compliance". In fact, this may be illustrated by a number of examples in the history of diplomacy. In the history of European integration we could recall the problems with ratification of some treaties. For example, the failed referendum in Denmark over the Treaty on European Union (initially signed also by the representative of Denmark) led to the decision to exempt Denmark from complying with some of the norms included in the Maastricht Treaty, like the obligation to adopt the Euro.

Now I would like to look at the way the norms appear in political discourse. The concept of discourse I want to use in the present discussion has been explained in the first chapter. I will only repeat that using the term "discourse" I have in mind a network of concepts which are semantically linked and together reflect the way in which a specific object of reflection is grasped in social communication. It is the understanding of discourse that allows E. Laclau to say that " The basic hypothesis of a discursive approach is that the very possibility of perception, thought and action depends on the structuration of a certain meaningful field, which pre-exists any factual immediacy" (E.Laclau, 1995: 431). J.Milliken has offered probably the most concise definition of discourse in this sense as "a structure of meaning-in-use" (Milliken, 1999: 231). Also, referring to the earlier part of the present chapter, I understand discourse as the realm in which most of the instruments of socialization mentioned – education, religion, law – operate.

It is exactly the reason why – in specific social or political contexts – competing discourses can take place. As it happens, the level and quality of education, the way religion and its norms are involved in a given normative structure as well as attitudes to law, in a decisive way affect the discourse which shape the whole normative structure in the minds of people. Antje Wiener, describing normative structure, suggests that "the normative structure is constituted by discursive interventions that secure the (re)construction of values, norms and rules entailed in it" (Wiener, 2004:190). It means that the discourse offers both a certain orientation of politics and its justification. It can be also useful to recall the view of W. E. Connolly, who stressed that discourse is not just an instrument or medium of politics but a dimension of politics, "an institutionalised structure of meaning that channels political thought and action in certain directions" (Connolly, 1983: 3, 1).

From what has been said so far it is quite clear that the role of political discourse extends far beyond the communicative functions and is closely linked to political action. It means that a particular discourse has definite practical, behavioural consequences. This is why it is so important to pay attention to the concepts that are organizing the whole discourse. In the European integration discourse there are two concepts which compete for the role of organizing element in the discourse. As it has been shown earlier these concepts are: solidarity and democracy. Of course, this competition does not mean that putting one of those concepts into the role of an organizing element eliminates the other completely. But it does make a difference in the overall functions of the political system of the EU and its normative structure. Depending on the choice of the organizing element, the whole European integration discourse either creates mental and political conditions for further development of the European Union and its transformation toward a federal system – which opens the way for establishment of democracy in the EU – or creates conditions for maintaining its intergovernmental form of governance, which leads to an unavoidable democracy deficit. As it has been argued earlier the whole situation is quite paradoxical because in order to secure democracy in the EU, European integration discourse must be organized not around the concept of democracy but around the concept of solidarity.

It is clear that in many cases norms are contested because they conflict with the norms that are accepted in a given society. Such situations seem to be quite natural in the process of European integration aimed at – among many other objectives – some kind of cohesion of a supranational entity which is supposed to bring together different states, with their own history, cultural heritage and national specificities. For the present discussion, however, I want to refer to one of the crucial constitutional options that appears to contradict the values and corresponding norms of a nation state, on the one hand, and of a supranational polity on the other. These values are: the sovereignty of nation states and democracy in the EU. As it has been indicated in the earlier part of the present text, making democracy in the EU a reality would require a decision to limit the sovereignty of the Member States. Of course, such a relation between those two values (and corresponding norms) has been rooted in a quite specific political discourse. The discourse involving the centuries-old basic political concept of "sovereignty" together with the concept of democracy known from the contemporary liberal democracies. As it has been argued earlier both concepts contribute to the construction of a political discourse that is quite inadequate to the new political reality created by the unprecedented political experiment of European integration. In consequence the European integration discourse suffers permanent ambiguity stemming from the inherent conflict of its basic concepts, ideals and the corresponding norms. No one is ready to give up either the sovereignty of Member States or democracy as a basic principle of the European Union. In fact, it is very rarely that inevitable contemporary limits to traditionally understood sovereignty are openly admitted. Therefore we observe constant efforts of politicians and political scientists to accommodate both concepts in European integration discourse. Conceptual instruments that are used to do the job include such inventions as "pooled sovereignty", "multi-level governance" or "open method of coordination". Of course, those concepts have also some descriptive functions, grasping a variety of elements of the developing new political reality. Their role in a reality-construction task, however, is to restore the normative structure of the new international European setting in such a way that the conflict of norms arising can be eliminated and so a new discourse emerge. The attempts to save both concepts, loaded with the potential for conflict, led to the detachment of their normative and axiological aspects. In effect, in political practice – depending on the context, domestic or international – both concepts can lead to norms that are in different situations contested while at the same time the values behind them are taken for granted.

The inevitable clash of this new discourse with the traditional discourse of a nation state's ideal of sovereignty has been best illustrated by the debates that refer to the concept of the "national interest". The problem is not an assumption that there are different interests in an integrating Europe, since this is a trivial fact in any complex social or political entity. The key word is "national". It imposes a traditional frame that includes an assumption that the national interests of one country must inevitably be contradicted by the national interests of other countries. This framework also includes another assumption. It suggests that defence of supposedly threatened "national interests" is a condition of survival of the nation.

The question of what in a new European context will make a constitutive factor for the nation to exist is a separate issue. At this point it may be enough to say that nationality and national specificity will have to be perceived quite differently than in past centuries. What is already clear, though, is that in a new European setting preservation of a nation and its distinctiveness will not depend on Westphalian sovereignty but rather on maintaining and developing national culture, which can indeed become a part of a common European cultural heritage.

Chapter VII

Future oriented discourse and the theories of integration

Already for some time the discourse on European integration has absorbed theoretical reflection on this process. In the present chapter I attempt to answer the question of how far existing theories of European integration are useful for reflection about the future of the European Union. First, the most often cited theories like neofunctionalism, intergovernmentalism and liberal intergovernmentalism are analysed to determine their theoretical background and assumptions. In the following section I will try to show that the so called "theories of integration" are to a great extent just rationalizations of the historically experienced practice of European integration and each of them is focused on different aspects of this process. Therefore, it can be shown that their subjects are, in fact, different. I refer to my book on The Object of Knowledge in Social Sciences which was published in Polish in 1979, in which the distinction between an object of investigation and an object of knowledge had been elaborated (Niżnik, Józef, 1979). In conclusion, I argue that existing theories of European integration are useless for any predictions concerning the future of the European Union. Therefore, reflection on the future of the EU calls for genuine creativity and new ideas. Some suggestions regarding this issue have been formulated at the end of the chapter.

Confronted with the ambitions of the students of European integration to develop its theory one has to ask why European integration should need a theory. Or, what such a theory can be used for. After all European integration has been a process that started in international politics in post-war Europe with quite specific intentions, goals and measures which have been explicitly formulated by appropriate actors, and concrete steps to achieve them have been undertaken. In other words, we are talking about a political reality which had its initiators (e.g. R. Schumann. J. Monnet, K. Adenauer and others), which has emerged as a result of political decisions and which has materialized in the form of international treaties. Does such a process need further explanation to be supplied by "theory"? Shouldn't we limit our interest just to the history of European integration? There is also a problem with justifying attempts to formulate a general theory of the EU. Simon Hix, cited by Ben Rosamond, formulated objections to such ambitions quite clearly: "We do not have a general theory of American or German politics so why should there be a general theory of the EU?" (Rosamond 2000; 17). Developing a "theory" of European integration may be perceived as a way to turn a specific flow of events, that is political decisions and their consequences, into an autonomous "object", detaching it from the will of people and placing it above the real current of politics. In other words, European integration might appear to be an Hegelian force (spirit) directing the activities of people. Among the variety of possible answers to the question formulated at the beginning there are two which seem to be especially relevant in the present discussion. First, European integration can possibly be used as a pattern for regional integration which could be followed in other parts of the world. Therefore, the theory of European integration could serve as a general theory of regional integration. Although such a role may seem to be confirmed by integrative initiatives on other continents there are serious objections which point out the specificity of the European context and its process of integration (Wallace, 1994). Also, the cases of integration elsewhere have never achieved the European level of integration. Another answer to the question of why should we need a theory of integration might be that such a theory would help us to predict the future of European integration which means also the future of the European Union.

In the present part of my study I would like to show that such expectations are totally unfounded. Let me start with initial reflections devoted to the future as the subject of academic research in the social sciences.

The future, as an object of research, is a case of a clearly unscientific subject (since the future does not exist at the time of reflection) which scientists do not want to give up. Moreover popular expectations addressed to science will not allow it to be given up. Reflection on the future of Europe seems to be an especially good illustration of the peculiarity of the theoretical status of future-oriented research. Social scientists undertaking so called "future studies" are in an especially difficult situation because, in addition to the peculiarity of their subject (the future), they have to face also the specificity of their disciplines, sociology, political science etc. The specificity of social sciences includes theoretical problems as well as the meanings of the basic epistemological categories and ontological distinctions. For example, the opposition "objective-subjective" must take into consideration the dual position of human beings in the process of cognition of social reality (Berger and Luckmann, 1966). However, despite theoretical problems with reflection about the future in social and political matters such reflection is indispensable for current decision-making and for justification of the corresponding actions.

It is quite natural that dealing with questions about the future we expect to profit from the relevant theories. In the social sciences, however, such expectation may appear groundless because of the very limited predictive potential of social theories. One should not be confused by the idea of predictive capability which, according to methodologists, is supposed to be one of the main features of any theory, along with capabilities to describe and to explain. First, those characteristics have been formulated with the natural sciences in mind, and – second – in the philosophy of science prediction has usually had a very "technical" meaning which need not necessarily be suitable for social matters which usually have a more complex nature than the subjects of the natural sciences. Therefore, for most of philosophers of science it is clear that "theory" in the social sciences is of a very "soft" kind. The sociologist, Jonathan Turner, puts this in the following words: "Any analysis of sociological theory should begin with a blunt admission that, from the perspective of ideal scientific theory, sociological theorizing has a long way to go" (Turner 1974; 8). The theorizing of political science seems to be in exactly the same situation. Use of theories of integration as a possible support for reflection about the future of the EU appears to be still more complicated, because those theories are even more distant from the ideal of scientific theory than most social theories.

In the following part of the chapter I will briefly analyse the process of cognition in the social sciences focusing on the theoretical status of theory and the nature of knowledge obtained in those disciplines. My aim at this point is to show that – if certain basic methodological requirements are observed – different social theories, even those competing for the status of the most correct ones, may in fact be rather complementary than rivals. Epistemological arguments for this thesis are usually either neglected or deliberately missed due to the variety of interests usually involved in social matters. European integration studies are an especially good area of political science to illustrate this situation. I will attempt to show that different theories of integration are just forms of "theorizing ex-post", that is theorizing about a process that has been accomplished. Such work might be justified if the aim of the theory were just explanation. However, "theories of integration" are also used to formulate visions of the future of Europe. Therefore, it is important to stress that such theorizing mostly serves predefined views on the future of an integrated Europe and are built on the basis of presumptions which reflect specific interests and preferences. In consequence, different theories can claim cognitive validity while offering competing ideas of European integration. Therefore, theories of integration are of little help in reflection on the future of the EU. In order to explain how is it possible that two competing theories may both be correct I have proposed to distinguish between an object of investigation (which may be common for different theories), and an object of knowledge (which may be different in the case of different theories).

The epistemological apparatus proposed in the next section helps to explain how it is possible to study the same object (an object of investigation) and to obtain knowledge which corresponds only to some of the possible aspects of this object. My suggestion is that the object covered by the acquired knowledge and explained by the relevant theory should be identified as an object different from the intended object of investigation. It is what I want to call an object of knowledge . Therefore, different theories of the same object of investigation (in our case it is European integration) may be, actually, instances of theorizing about different objects of knowledge.

The whole network of epistemological relations has been presented below in the diagram taken from my 1979 publication (Niżnik, 1979).

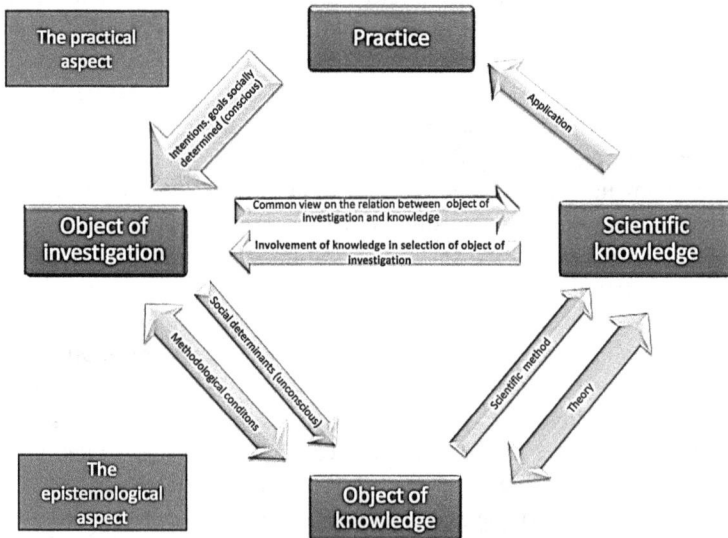

The upper part of the diagram presents the practical aspect, and the lower one the epistemological aspect of the process of knowledge creation (the process of cognition) in the social sciences. The practical aspect refers to common, every-day thinking about relation between scientific knowledge, its practical applications and the initiation of further research. According to such an approach scientific knowledge can be applied in practice and whenever new problems or new goals appear – in practice or within the body of knowledge already available – further questions and research tasks are formulated for the researchers. In this way their object of investigation (object of research) is designated. As a starting point for choosing (or designating) an object for research existing knowledge is used. It is clear that also at this stage that different elements of knowledge at hand, as well as different theories may be used and already at the start of the process of inquiry the attention of the researcher may be directed toward specific aspects of the selected object of investigation (but such observation requires some kind of epistemological awareness which in a common sense approach is usually absent). Nevertheless, the common assumption is that the results of research would add new elements to existing scientific knowledge about the investigated object.

Such a simplified view of the process of origin of scientific knowledge over-looks a number of factors which can be identified if the epistemological aspect of this process is taken into consideration. This aspect includes some of the findings of philosophy of science and sociology of knowledge. First, epistemo-logical analysis points out that research is conducted in specific "methodological conditions". This means a specific paradigm which includes a specific concep-tual apparatus (Kuhn 1970). In addition to those conditions there are other, mostly unconscious, factors which have their impact on the researcher embark-ing upon a particular research task; such as personal preferences, biographical experience or the social context of the research undertaken. It is clear that their influence is especially strong in the social sciences. The perception of the object of investigation by a particular researcher is determined by all those factors and – in effect – her/his attention is focused on a specific aspect of this object. So, the knowledge obtained refers to a quite different object than the one that had been designated (usually in general terms) although this difference is usually unnoticed since we tend to be blind to certain aspects of reality (Wittgenstein 2000 ; 298-299). Therefore, what can be reached in the process of cognition is an object of knowledge, which corresponds only to one of the possible aspects of the object of investigation. However, in every-day thinking the whole epistemological analysis needed to see those limits is usually absent. This is why the knowledge obtained used to be accepted as the truth about the object of investigation. In consequence, if in the whole process the rules of scientific method are observed, such knowledge is added to the existing body of knowledge and becomes the basis for a theory. It is then quite possible that different or even contradicting theories of the "same" object (phenomenon, process etc.) can all be correct. The fact that they, actually, are instances of theorizing on different objects (of knowledge) may be completely overlooked for a variety of reasons and in some cases deliberately covered up.

Let me now move to European integration, the subject which became an object of investigation for a number of political scientists conducting EU studies which resulted in different theories. Those theories usually compete with each other, although attempts to reconcile their differences are also present in some of the theoretical proposals (Peterson 1995, Richardson 1996). With all the limitations and restrictions that make the term "theory" in social sciences a kind of overstatement (if compared with theory in the natural sciences), the situation with theories of integration seems to be still more problematic. It has been shown in a number of analyses (Rosamond 2000; 189, Eilstrup-Sangiovanni 2006), and will be also argued further on in the present text, that theories of integration have a definite contextual character. This means that they have originated in specific historical circumstances, reflect specific approaches to politics and especially represent quite a clear stand with regard to the role of a nation state.

Political scientists discussing "theories of integration" are far from unanimous in their understanding of what should be counted as theorizing about European integration. Depending on the scope of their analyses they either present numerous theoretical approaches to integration (Rosamond 2000, Eilstrup-Sangiovanni 2006) or concentrate on just a few major positions in this area corresponding to the most intensely debated answers to the question of what kind of political entity the European Union is (Pollack 2005). Probably the best known, and indeed an excellent book on the topic, is Ben Rosamond's book on Theories of European Integration (Rosamond, 2000). Rosamond, unlike most other specialists on European integration, demonstrates a high level of awareness of the variety of factors determining the nature and the content of so called "theories of integration". He has kept a reasonable distance from the very use of the concept of "theory" in the context of European integration. Also, his extensive references to sociology of knowledge make his discussion of theories of integration a fascinating excursion into methodology and philosophy of the social sciences. At the same time, however, in a relatively concise text Rosamond in a very readable way builds quite a comprehensive landscape of conceptualizations of European integration. Concentrating on the first line of controversies in this area, those which have appeared in the debate between neofunctionalism and intergovernmentalism, Rosamond discusses also a number of other theoretical attempts which show that coexistence or even complementarity of those dominant rivals in theory of integration is possible. I was especially attracted to this book because I discovered that more than twenty years after my book on The Object of Knowledge in the Social Sciences was published (only in Polish, which makes it impossible for Rosamond to know it) someone has presented an almost identical view on the nature of the social sciences, referring to the same constitutive factors and using the same arguments.

Let me now recall the basic ideas of those major "theories of integration" . One should notice that the conceptualizations used can be quite misleading. For example, the term "neofunctionalism" suggests close links to functionalism.

Only more detailed analysis of the ideas of Ernst Haas, which formed the basis of neofunctionalism, and comparison with the works of David Mitrany, the leading figure in functional theory of integration, can show that their views on the nature of European integration are radically different. One of the main differences has been pointed out well by Rosamond, who suggests, that "Functionalism was primarily a theory of *post-territorial* governance, whereas neofunctionalism was an early theory of *regionalism*" (Rosamond 2000; 69).

Another source of confusions can be the term "intergovernmentalism". In the current European debate this term most often refers to one of the general approaches to European integration. It can serve as a description of the EU governance system stressing its (supposedly) basic mechanism of decision-making. In another use it can indicate the intentions of political leaders with regard to the preferable – or in some cases exclusively acceptable – form of relations between the EU Member States, which excludes or radically limits the role of supranational authority in these relations. However, the works on "theories of integration" use the word "intergovernmentalism" as a "theory" which attempts to answer the question 'what is the nature of European integration' or, in other words, of what is European integration (or European Union) an instance .

I would like now move to a more systematic, although very brief presentation of the main "theories of integration". European integration from the very beginning, that is since the European Coal and Steel Community was founded, undermined – by its very idea – the state-centred approach to politics. The tension between this most established view on international politics and the new forms of political relations which were initiated with the beginning of European integration, is probably the most important factor in the development of theories of integration and in theoretical disputes over the nature of the whole process. With the progress of integration the simplest and most basic distinctions became problematic. For example, what is "domestic" and what is "international"? Ben Rosamond quite extensively discusses the basic question whether International Relations is the proper discipline for studying European integration (Rosamond 2000; 157). There is no doubt that EU studies located on the basis of IR have been most often framed in an intergovernmental approach, because the main subject of this discipline is relations between the states. Some authors believe that IR might be the right discipline for studying the process of integration, and especially its initiation, but must be replaced by comparative politics when analysis of the EU system is taking place. Indeed, intergovernmentalism reflects the state-centric approach and its main problem is the position of the state and its role within an integrating totality. Within such an approach the problem of the nature of the EU political system seems to be falsely formulated since the only recognized actors in the politics of the EU are the Member States.

Neofunctionalism – on the other hand – concentrating on the process of integration itself, has been from the very beginning focused on the supranational powers and competences of the emerging political system. This is why neofunctionalism used, sometimes, to be identified with federalism.

It should be noted that what have been accepted as theoretical ideas on European integration were, in fact, instances of theorizing ex-post about empirical processes that had already been in progress. Ernst Haas's first book on European integration – published after the first years of experience of the European Coal and Steel Community at the moment when the next step of integration had been initiated – had immediate reference to practice at the start of the European Economic Community (Haas, 1958). Also, it looked like a correct theory because the initiation of the EEC had been perceived as a confirmation of the idea of a spill-over which, according to neofunctionalism, was a crucial mechanism of integration.

The next observation which can be made at this point is that representatives of different theoretical orientations start with different premises while seemingly attempting to answer the same or similar questions. However, if formulated on the ground of different premises the same questions usually open quite different areas of possible answers. For example, Rosamond points out, that Stanley Hoffmann who presented an early critique of neofunctionalism and opened a theoretical venue for the intergovernmental view on integration had perceived economics and politics as quite separate. On the other hand the strong linkage of the two has been the basic assumption of the neofunctional approach of Haas, Lindberg, and others. Therefore, theorizing on the basis of different assumptions most probably leads to different theoretical positions. As it will be shown later such different theoretical positions address in fact different objects of knowledge. In other words, from the very beginning those authors aimed to prove some of their initial theses which were different and – as long as the dissimilarity of their objects of knowledge was not noticed – might look contradictory.

The initial success of neofunctional reasoning could be attributed to its fundamental premises which relied on common beliefs and observations. For example neofunctionalists suggested that economic integration would inevitably lead towards political integration. There are enough everyday observations to assure us that there is no such thing as a purely economic process, completely detached from politics. Therefore, such an assumption must have looked quite convincing. The same applies to the idea of "spillover", the fundamental mechanism which, according to neofunctionalism, has been pushing integration further forward. In fact, this idea has been so much a part of common knowledge that in many languages it is expressed in proverbs. For example, in Polish there is a proverb saying: "if you give him a finger, he will grab the hand". According to the "spillover hypothesis" integration in one sector of the economy – due to the obvious functional links – would inevitably push integration in other sectors, and integration in the economy would spillover into politics. The beginning of European integration looked exactly like implementation of this rule. The initial six partners of ECSC within 6 years moved from coordination of steel and coal production toward further economic cooperation within the European Economic Community. In addition, the political aspirations of this next Community were quite explicit despite the "economic" name of the new organization. Although economic spillover was supposed to work by itself, it needed some measures of coordination which made necessary the emergence of a supranational authority with clear political competences. Moreover, the process of integration affects the mentality and attitudes of important figures in Member States leading to the "loyalty transference" which is necessary if the new supranational institutions are to function properly. Such loyalty transference can be easily explained and justified by the neofunctional belief that the main aim of the process is the welfare and well being of the people involved which can be better secured by a new form of international coexistence and cooperation. In this situation the distinction between what is "domestic" and what is "international" had to fade out. Of course, empirical research, for example that on national identity, made criticism of neofunctionalism an easy task. But careful analysis of the rival "theory" shows that the main reason for opposing neofunctionalism can be found at the level of initial assumptions, political beliefs and values. In other words, those who reject the neofunctional perspective on European integration are looking for a "theory of integration" which develops their different presumptions and supports their specific value structure.

The intergovernmental opposition to neofunctionalism, best represented by the works of Stanley Hoffman (1964, 1966), has been stimulated by assumptions and questions which did not bother the representatives of neofunctionalism . First of all there is the question which later acquired French expression of "*finalité*", that is the question of where the whole process of integration is heading, or of what the final form the new political system might take. The intergovernmental view from the very beginning was determined by a strong realist position regarding the nature of international politics in which the leading role was supposed to be played by the states. Therefore any development which might change this role had been rejected as unrealistic. In the background one can find a strong attachment to the value of the – traditionally understood – sovereignty of states discussed in an earlier chapter . With such a starting point it is easy to find arguments pointing to the weaknesses of the spill-over hypothesis or to question the idea of dependence between the economy and politics. In consequence, the intergovernmental approach was not so much interested in integration as a way to weaken or even only modify the role of states but in integration as a new environment for the state's actions in which Member States remain the basic actors. In other words, both "theories" pretending to grasp the same subject – European integration – have been referring to knowledge about different aspects, which in the end reflected different objects of knowledge. While neofunctionalism indeed tried to look for a new quality in this international experiment, intergovernmentalism was interested in the challenges which this experiment created for the states and any hypothesis that would take into consideration the transfer of power to a supranational authority was rejected at the start.

Andrew Moravcsik, with his liberal intergovernmentalism, added still more complications to the understanding of this concept. Moving his attention from the decision-making processes of the EU to the factors that decide about Member States' positions in intergovernmental bargaining, Moravcsik stressed the importance of domestic matters for common decisions in the EU. His liberal intergovernmentalism simply takes into consideration the impact of the domestic politics of Member States on the process of European integration. Moravcsik suggests, that "An understanding of domestic politics is a precondition for, not a supplement to, the analysis of strategic interaction among states", (Moravcsik, 1993; 481). Putting "European integration" in the place of "strategic interaction among states" here opens a very useful venue for explanation of a variety of episodes in the history of European integration, which took place only because of the domestic issues of some member states . One recent example is the failure of the ratification process of the European Constitution in France and the Netherlands in referenda in 2005. What makes Moravcsik's idea still more confusing is the fact that, depending on the way his arguments are used, liberal intergovernmentalism can also be read – probably against the intentions of its author – as a support for neofunctionalism. For example, it is quite possible that sometimes domestic pressure can be in favour of spill-over, if extending integration into further sectors of the economy or public life would seem to be beneficial for the particular state. Also, Moravcsik's opinion on democratic legitimacy in the European Union can serve as a kind of support for neofunctional logic: he believes that there is no problem of democratic deficit in the EU because, after all, decisions in the European Council are made by representatives of Member States who are democratically elected in their countries. In fact, the idea of a "two-level game" – gaining domestic support for actions that are instrumental for integration (international dimension), which can then stimulate behaviour of the electorate favourable for domestic politicians – can be also perceived as an argument useful for bridging the gap between intergovernmentalism and neofunctionalism (Putnam, 1988).

Therefore, those "theories" should not be perceived as competing paradigms. In their backgrounds we can easily find different leading questions ("What is the role of the nation state in an integrating Europe?" vs. "Why and how is the process of integration progressing?"), stemming from different conceptions of acceptable political settings ("A Member State's position must not be undermined by supranational institutions" vs. "the common interest of integrated Europe reflects the best interests of Member States"), referring to different structures of values (Westphalian vs. post-Westphalian). Of course this last difference, indeed, indicates competing views on the main political objectives. But those views are not the results of different theories but of initial premises which determine political preference, and in consequence lead to separate "theories". Therefore, Ben Rosamond is right when he states, that "intergovernmentalism is a *political preference* held by a range of actors within the EU" (Rosamond 2000;153).

In order better to see the differences in the theoretical aims of both approaches one can simply ask questions about certain theoretical or logical inconsistencies. One such question, addressed to intergovernmentalism, is: "why do states participate in activity which limit their autonomy?". Of course, there is a number of possible answers which may refer to quite different theories. The "two-level game" discussed earlier is one of them. The very question, however, as well as the possible answers show that intergovernmentalism needs also other approaches, not excluding those that have been declared as rival theories, in order to solve different puzzles that have been created by the process of European integration. In the case of this particular question a supporter of intergovernmentalism might simply answer that the states participate in the process of integration only as far as their autonomy is not threatened. Such an answer would not be satisfactory because the limits imposed by the process of integration on the state's autonomy are too visible even if decision-making procedures seem to be based on intergovernmental bargaining as a fundamental mechanism. More satisfactory would be an answer which, in fact, needs a neofunctional approach to integration: the states participate in integration for reasons which may be in each case different but in every case this participation serves their particular goals of some kind.

The way European integration is conceptualised in the intergovernmental approach indicates a kind of "conceptual inertia" (Niznik 1979; 106). The deep-rooted concepts – like "state" or "sovereignty", for example – have been redefined because of the pressure of current political reality but some remains of their old, outdated meanings, are still present.

The problems with conceptualization of the current political reality in the integrating Europe have led to some terminological inventions which took for granted what had been observed in the EU, and on the basis of the current political practice created conceptual and theoretical novelties. This is the case with the idea of Multi-Level Governance or with the Open Method of Coordination (Niznik, 2006; 8). Both ideas fit well into a new approach to the developing political reality in the EU, which has been diagnosed as a "governance turn" in EU studies. The first one clearly intends – within the so called "governance turn" in EU studies – to pacify the controversy over federal (neofunctional at bottom) or intergovernmental courses of EU development. The latter offers a solution in such cases of policy-making when there is a need for a common policy but existing legal provisions leave the right of decision to the Member States' governments. The development of such conceptual inventions show that existing "theories of integration" are unable to grasp the full specificity of European processes of integration. Therefore, we should not expect that such inadequate "theories" would be helpful in predicting the future of the European Union, which will be determined by a variety of factors of both internal and external origin.

What is the real meaning of the "governance turn" in EU studies? This was not a turn in style of theorizing or a turn in theoretical preferences, but a move toward a different problem area. And the reason for this move was not theoretical dissatisfaction with one theory or another but an opening to a different aspect of the process of integration that came together with the Treaty on the EU. At the same time, however, this turn –with the MLG idea – created an alternative to the state-centred perspective of the intergovernmental approach to the European integration. In this way MLG has been sometimes perceived as a replacement for neofunctionalism, which certainly is not the case. The governance turn reflects only a change of the object of knowledge in EU studies, and not the replacement of one theory of integration with another one. In fact, such a "turn" could be understood as an empirical solution to at least one dilemma in the theoretical debate over European integration: the question whether the European Union is one of the known forms of political phenomena (e.g. an international organization) or is a "*sui generis*" political system. Moving to the centre of EU studies, the phenomenon of governance seems to confirm the idea of the European Union as a "*sui generis*" political entity. In fact, such confirmation may be found also in the views of informed politicians. Denis MacShane, a former British Minister for Europe, commenting on the 2009 election of the President of the European Commission, characterized this position in the following words: "In theory it's one of the most powerful jobs in the world. But this is Europe, where the normal rules don't apply" (MacShane, 2009).

Therefore, speculating about the future of the EU on the basis of existing "theories" – which are mostly ex-post rationalizations of some aspects of integration practice – does not look very promising. The phenomenon of the European Union calls for genuinely creative ideas which would go beyond the current controversy over federalism versus intergovernmentalism (Niżnik, 2007). The future of the EU seems to depend mostly on the wisdom of Europeans. Unfortunately, so far, there are no signals of a surplus of wisdom in Europe. On the contrary, in the Member States' public debates European matters most often appear in the framework of local politics for which "the European interest" is too abstract an idea. It is clear that the lack of thinking in terms of "European interests" makes us blind to many opportunities that European integration may offer. Although global challenges have made their way into the public discourse there is no common awareness of the fact that global threats can be more easily controlled by common policies and institutions. There are more elements in the most acceptable vision of contemporary politics and social life which are basic and important but their role in the discourse about European integration is mistaken. For example, the elevation of the ideal of democracy to the position of an absolute value and an organizing element of the whole European discourse made it very difficult for people to accept the role of elites. Also, the paramount importance of democracy has imposed on the European discourse a very specific structure of sense which has pushed to the side other values which at the beginning of the European integration process served as the leading ideals (Niżnik, 2008). Probably the most important of them is solidarity, which is still present in the European discourse but most often as the object of lip service.

Concluding, I would like to recall Michael Burgess's reference to Spinelli suggesting that the European Union "is the product of the interaction between what exists and what must exist" (Michael Burgess, 2000; 280). Everything indicates, that we underestimate the role of "what must exist" and what probably will be a decisive factor in the future development of the EU, e.g. a global reshuffling of the world scene which will force Europeans to a deeper unity. Therefore, although theories of integration might be only a kind of intellectual exercise and offer very little to predict the future of the EU, we certainly need further theorizing in order to get the best from what is inevitable anyway: a more integrated Europe, proud of its diversities but also with a stronger common identity of Europeans.

Bibliography

Amin, Ash (2004), Multi-Ethnicity and the Idea of Europe, Theory, Culture & Society, vol.21, no.2, pp.1-24.

Anderson, B. (1991), Imagined Communities: Reflections on the Origin and Spread of Nationalism, London, Verso.

Anderson, John (1999), Post-industrial Solidarity or Meritocracy?, Acta Sociologica, vol.42, no.2 pp.375-385.

Arnsperger, Christian and Varoufakis, Yanis (2003), Toward A Theory of Solidarity, Erkenntnis, vol.59, no 2, pp. 157- 188.

Arts Wil and Gelissen, John (2001), Welfare States, Solidarity and Justice Principles: Does the Type Really Matter?, Acta Sociologica,.

Baczko, Bronisław (1997), Models of the Citizen During the French Revolution, in: Wykłady Inauguracyjne 1993-1996, Zeszyty Szkoły Nauk Społecznych no.2, Warszawa, pp. 95-105.

Balibar, Etienne, (1996), Fictive Ethnicity and Ideal Nation, in: John Hutchinson & Anthony D. Smith (eds.), Ethnicity, Oxford University Press, Oxford, pp.164-168.

Ball Terence (1988), Transforming Political Discourse. Political Theory and Critical Conceptual History", Basil Blackwell, Oxford.

Bauman, Zygmunt (1997), Glokalizacja, czyli komu globalizacja, a komu lokalizacja," Studia Socjologiczne, no 3(146).

Beck, Urlich and Grande, Edgar, (2007), Cosmopolitanism: Europe's Way out of Crisis, in: European Journal of Social Theory, vol.10, Number 1, February, pp.67-86.

Berger, Peter L. and Luckmann, Thomas (1996), The Social Construction of Reality, Doubleday & Company, New York.

Bommes, Michael and Geddes, Andrew (eds.), 2000, Immigration and Welfare. Challenging the borders of the welfare state, Routledge, London.

Bottici, Chiara and Challand, Benoit, (2006), Rethinking Political Myth: The Clash of Civilizations as a Self-Fulfilling Prophecy, in: European Journal of Social Theory, vol.9, Number 3, August, pp.315-336.

Bovens, Mark (2006), Analysing and Assessing Public Accountability. A Conceptual Framework, EuroGov Paper: http://www.connex-network.org/eurogov/pdf/egp-connex-C-06-01.pdf.

Brown, David (2004), Why Independence? The Instrumental and Ideological Dimensions of Nationalism, in: International Journal of Comparative Sociology, vol. 45 no 3-4, pp.277-296.

Búrca, Gráinne, de (ed.), 2005, EU Law and the Welfare State. In Search of Solidarity, Oxford University Press, New York.

Búrca, Gráinne, de, 2005-2, Towards European Welfare, in: Búrca, Gráinne, de (ed.), EU Law and the Welfare State, pp.1-9.

Burgess, Michael (2000), Federalism and European Union: The Building of Europe, 1950-2000, Routledge, London.

Burnstein, Daniel, Euroquake (1991), Simon & Schuster, New York.

Camilleri Joseph A. and Jim Falk (1992) eds., The End of Sovereignty?, Edward Elgar, Aldershot.

Caminada Koen, Goudswaard Kees, Van Vliet Olaf, 2010, Pattern of Welfare State Indicators in the EU: Is there Convergence?, in: Journal of Common market Studies, vol.48, no.3, pp.529-556.

Cassirer, Ernst (1944), An Essay on Man. An Introduction to a Philosophy of Human Culture, Yale University Press, New Haven and London.

Cassirer, Ernst (1955), The Philosophy of Symbolic Forms, vol.I-III, Yale University Press.

Cederman, Lars-Eric, (2001), Nationalism and Bounded Integration: What it Would Take to Construct a European Demos, European Journal of International Relations, vol.7(2), pp.139-174.

Chernilo, Daniel, (2006), Social Theory's Methodological Nationalism: Myth and Reality, in: European Journal of Social Theory, vol.9, Number 1, February, pp.5-22.

Connolly, William E. (1983), The Terms of Political Discourse, Princeton University Press, Princeton.

Cousins, Mel, 2005, European Welfare States. Comparative Perspectives, Sage, London.

Dahl Robert A. (1989), Democracy and its Critics, Yale University Press, New Haven.

Daly, Mary, 2006, EU Social policy after Lisbon, in: Journal of Common market Studies, vol.44, no.3, pp.461– 481.

Davies Norman (1996), Europe. A History, Introduction, Oxford University Press, Oxford, New York.

Delanty, Gerard,(1995), Inventing Europe, Palgrave Macmillan, London.

Delanty, Gerard, and O'Mahony, Patrick, (2002), Nationalism and Social Theory, Sage Publications, London.

Deutsch, Karl W. (1967), Nationalism and Social Communication. An inquiry into the Foundations of Nationality, The M.I.T. Press, Cambridge and London.

Diamond, Larry and Plattner, Marc F. (2001), The Global Divergence of Democracies, The John Hopkins university Press, Baltimore and London.

Diez Thomas (1999), Speaking „Europe": the politics of integration discourse, in: Journal of European Public Policy, no.4, pp.598-613.

Diez Thomas (2001), Europe as a Discursive Battleground. Discourse Analysis and European Integration Studies, in: Cooperation and Conflict, vol.36 (1), Sage Publications.

Douglas, Arnold R. (2004), Congress, the Press, and Political Accountability, Princeton University Press, Princeton.

Dunkan, H.D. (1968), Symbols in Society, Oxford University Press, London-Oxford-New York.

Dzur, Albert W. (2002), Nationalism, Liberalism, and Democracy, in: Political Research Quarterly, vol.55, no 1, pp. 191-211.

Edelman Murray (1985), The Symbolic Uses of Politics, University of Illinois Press, Urbana and Chicago.

Eilstrup-Sangiovanni, Mette (ed.) (2006), Debates on European Integration, Palgrave, New York.

European Social Policy – A Way Forward for the Union . A White Paper (1994), http://europa.eu/documentation/official-docs/white-papers/pdf/social_policy_white_paper_com_94_333_a.pdf.

Ferrera, Maurizio, Rhodes, Martin (2002), Recasting European Welfare States, Frank Cass Publishers, London.

Ferrera, Maurizio (2005), Towards an 'Open' Social Citizenship? The New Boundaries of Welfare in the European Union, in: Búrca, Gráinne, de (ed.), EU Law and the Welfare State, pp. 11-38.

Ferrera, Maurizio (2005),The Boundaries of Welfare. European Integration and the New Spatial Politics of Social Protection, Oxford University Press, Oxford-New York.

Fine, Robert and Boon, Vivienne, (2007), Cosmopolitanism: Between Past and Future, in: European Journal of Social Theory, vol.10, Number 1, February, pp.5-16.

Fine, Robert, (2003), Taking the "Ism' out of Cosmopolitanism: An Essay in Reconstruction, in: European Journal of Social Theory, vol.6, Number 4, November, pp.451-470.

Foucault, Michel (1972), The Archaeology of Knowledge and the Discourse on Language, Pantheon Books, New York.

Freeden, Michael (1996), Ideologies and Political theory. A Conceptual Approach, Oxford, Oxford University Press.

Gallie, Walter Bryce (1962), Essentially Contested Concepts, in: Max Black, The Importance of Language, Prentice-Hall, Inc., Englewood Cliffs, N.J.

Galtung Johan (1994), The Emerging European Supernationalism, in: Max Haller, Rudolf Richter (eds.), Toward a European Nation?, M.E.Sharpe, London, pp.212-225.

Gellner E., (1983), Nations and Nationalism, Basil Blackwell Ltd., Oxford.

Giddens, Anthony (1990), The Consequence of Modernity, Polity Press, Cambridge.

Giddens, Anthony (1991), Modernity and Self-Identity: Self and society in the late modern age, Polity Press, Cambridge.

Giordano, Benito and Roller, Elisa (2002), Catalonia and the 'Idea of Europe'. Competing Strategies and Discourses within Catalan Party Politics, in: European Urban and Regional Studies, vol.9, no 2, pp.99-113.

Greve, Bent (2003), Introduction: The End of the Welfare State?, The European Legacy, vol.8, No 5, pp. 557- 558.

Greve, Bent (2003-2), Way Forward for the Welfare State in the Twenty-first Century, The European Legacy, vol.8, No 5, pp.611-630.

Haas, Ernst (1958), The Uniting Europe. Political, Social and Economic Forces, 1950-1957, Stanford University Press, Stanford.

Habermas Jürgen (1966), Between Facts and Norms. Contributions to a Discourse Theory of Law and Democracy, translated by William Rehg, MIT Press, Cambridge, Mass., p.329-387.

Habermas, Jürgen (1992), Citizenship and National Identity: Some Reflections on the Future of Europe, Praxis International, 12, pp. 1- 19.

Habermas, Jürgen (1993), Obywatelstwo a tożsamość narodowa, IFiS PAN, Warszawa

Hannerz, Ulf (1990), Cosmopolitans and Locals in World Culture, in: Mike Featherstone (ed.), Global Culture. Nationalism, Globalization and Modernity, Sage Publications, London.

Harlow, Carol and Eawlings, Richard (2006), Promoting Accountability in Multi-Level Governance: A Network Approach, EuroGove Paper, http://www.connex-network.org/eurogov/pdf/egp-connex-C-06-02.pdf.

Hechter, Michael, (2002), Containing Nationalism, Oxford University Press, New York.

Hedetoft, Ulf (1994), The State of Sovereignty in Europe: Political Concept or Cultural Self-Image, in: Staffan Zetterholm (ed.), National cultures and European Integration. Exploratory Essays on Cultural Diversity and Common Policies, Berg, Oxford – Providence, USA, pp.13- 48.

Heidenreich, Martin and Zeitlin, Jonathan, 2009, Changing European Employment and Welfare Regimes. The influence of the open method of coordination on national reforms, Routledge, New York.

Held, Klaus (1993), "Wise citizen" by Machiavelli, in: Barbara Markiewicz (ed.), Citizen: renaissance of the concept, (in Polish), IFiS Publishers, Warsaw.

Hermann Christoph and Hofbauer Ines (2007), The European social model: Between competitive modernization and neoliberal resistance, in: Capital& Class, Autumn, vol.31, no 3, pp. 125-139.

Hix Simon (1999), The Political System of the European Union, MacMillan Press Ltd., London, s.14-16.

Hoffmann, Stanley (1964), The European Process at Atlantic Cross -purposes, in: Journal of Common Market Studies, no.3.

Hoffmann, Stanley (1966), Obstinate or Obsolete? The Fate of the Nation State and the Case of Western Europe, in: Daedalus, 95.

Hollis, Martin Friends (1999), Romans and consumers, in: David Milligan, William Watts Miller. Liberalism, Citizenship and Autonomy, Arebury.

Hooghe Liesbet (2003), Europe Divided? Elites vs. Public Opinion on European Integration, Institute for Advanced Studies, Political Science Series, Vienna.

Huntington, Samuel P. (1996), The Clash of Civilisations and the Remaking of World Order, Simon & Schuster, New York.

Hülsse Rainer, (2006), Imagine the EU: the metaphorical construction of supra-nationalistist identity, Journal of International Relations and Development, 9, pp.396–421.

Jankowiak Janusz (1989), Jutro Europy, Tygodnik "Solidarność", nr.5 (42).

Jones, Catherine (ed.), 1993, New Perspectives on the Welfare State in Europe, Routledge, London- New York.

Kantner, Cathleen, (2006), Collective Identity as Shared Ethical Self-Understanding. The Case of the Emerging European Identity, in: European Journal of Social Theory, vol.9, Number 4, November, pp. 501–523.

Kennedy, Paul (1993), Preparing for the Twenty-First Century, Vintage Books, New York,

Kinander Morten (2007), The Accountability Function of Courts. A Methodological Framework for Inquiry, in: Niznik, Jozef and Ryabinska, Natalya (eds.) Political Accountability. Conceptual, Theoretical and Practical Dimensions, IFiS Publishers, Warsaw

King, Anthony, (2005), Towards a Transnational Europe: The case of the Armed Forces, in: European Journal of Social Theory, vol.8, Number 3, August, pp.321–340.

Klein, Rudolf, 1993, O'Goffe tale. Or what can we learn from the success of the capitalist welfare states, in: Jones, Catherine, New Perspectives.., pp.6–15.

Kritzinger, Sylvia, (2005), European Identity Building from the Perspective of Efficiency, Comparative European Politics, 3, pp.50-75.

Kuhn, Thomas (1970), The Structure of Scientific Revolutions, University of Chicago Press, Chicago.

Kuhnle, Stein (ed.), 2000, Survival of the European Welfare State, Routledge, New York.

Kuhnle, Stein, 2000, European welfare lessons of the 1990s, in: Kuhnle, Stein (ed.), Survival..., pp.234-238.

Kuus Merje, (2004), Europe's eastern expansion and reinscription of otherness in East-Central Europe, in: Progress in Human Geography vol.28, no 4, pp.472-489.

Kvist, Jon and Saari, Juho, 2007, The Europeanisation of social protection, The Policy Press, Bristol.

Laclau Ernesto (1995), Discourse in: Robert E. Goodin i Philip Pettit (eds.), A Companion to Contemporary Political Philosophy, Blackwell Publishers Ltd., Oxford-Cambridge, Mass.

MacShane, Denis (2009), The Accidental Head of Europe, in: Newsweek, September 21.

Markiewicz, Barbara (ed.) (1993), Citizen: renaissance of the concept, (in Polish), IFiS Publishers, Warsaw.

Martinsen, Dorte Sindbjerg, 2005, Social Security Regulation in the EU: The De-Territorialization of Welfare?, in: Búrca, Gráinne, de (ed.), EU Law and the Welfare State, pp. 89-110.

Martinsen, Dorte Sindbjerg, 2005-2, The Europeanisation of Welfare – The Domestic Impact of Intra-European Social Security, in: Journal of Common market Studies, vol.40, no.4, pp.1027-1054.

Mason, Andrew (2004), Community, Solidarity and Belonging. Levels of Community and Their Normative Significance, Cambridge University Press, Cambridge

Mikkeli, Heikki, (1998), Europe as an Idea and an Identity, MacMillan Press Ltd., New York, Nationalism, Federalism and the United States of Europe.

Moravcsik Andrew (2002), In Defense of the 'Democratic Deficit': Reassessing Legitimacy in the European Union, JCMS Volume 40, number 4, pp.603-24.

Morley D., and Robins, K., (1995), Spaces of Identity: Global media, electronic landscapes and cultural boundaries, Routledge, London.

Müller, Hans Peter (2000), Global Elites? Notes To A Poorly Defined Concept, in : Carlo Mongardini (ed.), Vecchie e nuove élites, Bulzoni Editore, Roma.

Niżnik, Józef (1979), Przedmiot poznania w naukach społecznych, PWN, Warszawa.

Niżnik, Józef (1985), Symbole, a adaptacja kulturowa (Symbols and Cultural Adaptation), Warsaw.

Niżnik, Józef (ed.) (1991), Postrzeganie Europy (Perception of Europe), Warsaw.

Niżnik, Józef and Skotnicka-Illasiewicz, Elżbieta (1992),What is Europe for Young Poles, in: International Journal of Sociology, vol.22, Nos.1-2, Spring – Summer pp.50-69.

Niżnik, Józef, (1993), Być obywatelem, w: Wartość bycia, wyd. Polskie Towarzystwo Filozoficzne, Kraków-Warszawa.

Niżnik, Józef (2000), National Identity and the Process of European Integration, in: Polish Sociological Review, no 4(132).

Niżnik, Józef (2002), The Europeans in Global Communication, in: Carlo Mongardini (ed.), La Civiltà Della Comunicazione Globale, Bulzoni Editore, Roma 2002, pp.81-92.

Niżnik, Józef (ed.) (2006 a), Multilevel Governance: Patterns and Degrees of Political Integration. The EU Eastern Enlargement Challenge, IFiS Publishers, Warsaw.

Niżnik, Józef (2006b), Integracja europejska w dyskursie politycznym, in: Jolanta Polakowska-Kujawa (Ed.), Współczesna Europa w procesie zmian, Difin, Warszawa 2006, pp. 33-64.

Niżnik, Józef (2006c), The Arbitrariness of Philosophy. An Essay on Metaphilosophical Functionalism, The Davies Group;Publishers, Aurora, Colorado.

Niżnik, Józef and Ryabinska, Natalya (eds.) (2007), Political Accountability. Conceptual, Theoretical and Practical Dimensions, IFiS Publishers, Warsaw.

Niżnik, Józef (2007), On Imperative of Creative Thinking about European Integration, in: Dialogue and Universalism, vol.XVII, no.12/2007.

Niżnik, Józef (2008), Discourse and Social Communication. The Case of "Democracy" in the European Integration Discourse, in: Josef Langer (ed.), Forces Shaping the EU. Social Science Approaches to Understanding the European Union, Peter Lang, 2008, Frankfurt am Main – Berlin – Bern- Bruxelles – New York- Oxford – Wien, pp.215-228.

Niżnik, Józef (2011a), Theories of Integration and the Future of the European Union, in: Josef Langer (ed.), Analysis and Visions for Europe, Peter Lang, Frankfurt am Main, pp. 19-30

Niżnik, Józef (2011b), The Concept of Solidarity in the European integration discourse, in: Marion Ellison (ed.), Reinventing social solidarity across Europe, The Policy Press, Bristol.

Peterson, John (1995), Decision –making in the European Union: Towards a Framework for Analysis, in: Journal of European Public Policy vol. 2(1).

Pollack, Mark (2005), Theorizing EU Policy Making, in: Helen Wallace, William Wallace and Mark A. Pollack, Policy-Making in the European Union, 5th edition, Oxford University Press, New York, 2005, pp. 13-48.

Pomian, Krzysztof (1990), L'Europe Et Ses Nations, Gallimard, Collection "Le Debat", Paris.

Potter Jonathan (1996), Representing reality. Discourse, Rhetoric and Social Construction, Sage Publications, London.

Putnam, Robert (1988), Diplomacy and Domestic Politics, in: International Organization, no.42.

Richardson, Jeremy (1996), Policy-making in the EU: Interests, Ideas and Garbage Cans of Primeval Soup, in: J.Richardson (ed.), European Union: Power and Policy-Making, Routledge, London.

Riedel, Manfred (1993), In search of "citizen ties" /Burgerbund/. The idea of political and the problem of European democracy, in B. Markiewicz (ed.), op.cit. pp.31- 44.

Rieffer, Barbara-Ann J. (2003), Religion and nationalism, in : Ethnicities, vol.3, no.2, pp.215-242.

Robyn, Richard (2004), ed., The Changing Face of European Identity: A Seven-nation Study of (Supra)national Attachments, Routledge, Oxford.

Rosamond, Ben (2000), Theories of European Integration, St. Martin Press, New York.

Rothstein, Bo,2000, The future of the universal welfare state: an institutional approach, in: Kuhnle, Stein (ed.), Survival..., pp.217 – 233.

Rothstein, Bo, 1998, Just institutions matter: the moral and political logic of the universal welfare state, Cambridge University Press, Cambridge.

Sadowski, Zdzisław (ed.) (1993), Post-totalitarian Society: The Course of Change, IFiS Publishers, Warsaw.

Sadowski, Zdzisław (1993), Economic and political consequences of disparities between national economies within the Common Economic Space and how to deal with them, in: Józef Niżnik (ed.), Unequal European Partnership, IFiS Publishers, Warsaw, pp. 57-62.

Sadurski W. (2006), European Constitutional Identity?, EUI Working Paper LAW, no.2006/33.

Scharpf, Fritz, 2002, The European Social Model, in: Journal of Common market Studies, vol.40, no.4, pp.645-670

Schuyt, Kees (1998), The Sharing of Risks and the Risks of Sharing: Solidarity and Social Justice in the Welfare State, Ethical Theory and Moral Practice, no.1, pp.297-311.

Schwilk Heimo (1997), Spiritual Foundation of Europe (Duchowy fundament Europy), Rzeczpospolita, 18-19 X, no.244/1997.

Sen Amartya (2001), Democracy as a universal value, in: Larry Diamond and marc F.Plattner (eds.), The Global Divergence of Democracies, The John Hopkins University Press, Baltimore and London.

Shore, Cris, (2004), Whither European Citizenship? Eros and Civilization revisited, in: European Journal of Social Theory, vol.7, Number 1, February, pp. 27 – 44.

Simonsen, Kirsten (2004), 'Europe', National Identities and Multiple Others, in: European Urban and Regional Studies, vol.11 no 4, pp. 357 – 362.

Smith, Anthony D. (1991), National Identity, Penguin Books.

Smith, Antony D. (2003), Nationalism, Polity Press, Cambridge (Polish edition: Sic!, 2007).

Smith, Dan (2000), Ethical Uncertainties of Nationalism, in: Journal of Peace Research, vol. 37, no.4, pp.489 – 502.

Soysal, Nuhoglu Yasemin (1996), Changing Citizenship in Europe. Remarks on postnational membership and the national state, in: David Cesarani and Mary Fulbrook (eds.), Citizenship, Nationality and Migration in Europe, London and New York, Routledge, 1996, pp.17- 29.

Stjernø, Steinar (2005),Solidarity in Europe. The History of an Idea, Cambridge University Press, Cambridge p.199.

Stråth, Bo, (2002), A European Identity: To the Historical Limits of a Concept, European Journal of Social Theory, 5, pp.387- 401.

Tomlinson, John (1991), Cultural Imperialism. A Critical Introduction, Pinter Publishers, London.

Tomlison, John (1999), Globalization and Culture, Polity Press, Cambridge.

Turner, Jonathan (1974), The Structure of Sociological Theory, The Dorsey Press, Homewood, Illinois.

Wallace, William (1994), Regional Integration: The West European Experience, Brooking Institution, Washington D.C.

Wallerstein, Immanuel (1991), The National and the Universal: Can there be such a thing as world culture? in: Anthony D. King (ed.), Culture, Globalisation and the World System, Macmillan, London.

Warleigh, Alex (2006), Learning from Europe? EU Studies and Re-thinking of "International Relations", in: European Journal of International Relations, vol.12 (1).

Weale, Albert, 1994, Social Policy and European Union, Social Policy & Administration, vol.28, no.1, pp.5-19.

Webster's II New Riverside University Dictionary (1984), The Riverside Publishing Company, Boston.

What is the European Social Model?, 2008, Social Europe Journal, vol.4, Issue 1, Autumn.

Widegren, Örjan(1997), Social Solidarity and Social Exchange, Sociology,vol.31/4, pp.755-771.

Wieviorka, Michel, (1995), The Ethnicity Triangle, in: Aleksandra Ålund and Raol Granqvist (eds.), Negotiating Identities, Rodopi, Amsterdam-Atlanta, GA, pp.33 – 43.

Wittgenstein, Ludwig (1997), Philosophical Investigations, Blackwell Publishers, Oxford UK, Part two, chapter XI.

Wittgenstein, Ludwig (2000), Philosophical Investigations, Polish edition: Dociekania Filozoficzne, PWN Warszawa.

Van Dijk Teun A., ed., (1997) Discourse as Structure and Process, Sage Publications, London.

Zeitlin, Jonathan, 2005, Social Europe and Experimentalist Governance: Towards a new Constitutional Compromise?, in: Búrca, Gráinne, de (ed.), EU Law and the Welfare State, pp. 213 – 241.

Zetterholm, Staffan (1994) Why is Cultural Diversity a political problem? A Discussion of Barriers to political Integration, in: Staffan Zetterholm (ed.), National Culture and European Integration. Exploratory Essays on Cultural Diversity and Common Policies, Berg, Oxford, 1994, pp. 65 – 82.

Studies in European Integration, State and Society

Edited by Góra Magdalena, Mach Zdzisław and Zielińska Katarzyna

Vol. 1   Józef Niżnik: Democracy versus Solidarity in the EU Discourse. 2012.

www.peterlang.de

Yongha Kim / György Széll (eds.)

Economic Crisis and Social Integration

Frankfurt am Main, Berlin, Bern, Bruxelles, New York, Oxford, Wien, 2011.
VIII, 275 pp., num. fig., tables and graphs
Comparative Regional Integration Studies.
Edited by György Széll and Woosik Moon. Vol. 1
ISBN 978-3-631-62059-5 · hb. € 44,80*

The Korea Institute for Health and Social Affairs (KIHASA) organised an international symposium on the economic crisis and social integration, which took place in Seoul on May 27–28, 2009. At the symposium took part besides researchers from KIHASA representatives from Ireland, France, England, Germany, Denmark, The Netherlands, the USA, Japan and China. This book assembles most of these contributions. This volume is absolutely up to date as the economic crisis is far from overcome and social reintegration remains one of the foremost challenges in today's world.

Content: How are Social Policies in the EU Responding to the Financial Crisis? · Social Protection for the Economic Crisis: The US Experience · China's Social Policy Choices in Times of the World Financial Crisis · Weathering the Storm: Consociational Democracy and Crisis Management in the Netherlands · Social Policy Stability in Times of Economic Crisis: The Case of Germany · Crisis Governance in Denmark: Is Flexicurity Delivering? Policy Tasks for Social Integration in Times of the Economic Crisis: the Case of South Korea · The Relationship between the Economic Crisis, Non-regular labourers, and Social Security in Present-day Japan · The Current Status of Health Insurance and Tasks Ahead · Efficient Management of Medical Treatment Costs of the Health Insurance for the Elderly · The Financial Crisis and its Impact on the Pension and Retirement Income System · Korean National Pensions: Facts and Functions in 2009

*The e-price includes German tax rate. Prices are subject to change without notice

Frankfurt am Main · Berlin · Bern · Bruxelles · New York · Oxford · Wien
Distribution: Verlag Peter Lang AG
Moosstr. 1, CH-2542 Pieterlen
Telefax 0041 (0)32/3761727
E-Mail info@peterlang.com

40 Years of Academic Publishing
Homepage http://www.peterlang.com